West Indian Cookery

E Phyllis Clark

Nelson Caribbean

Thomas Nelson and Sons Ltd
Nelson House Mayfield Road
Walton-on-Thames Surrey KT12 5PL
P.O. Box 18123 Nairobi Kenya

Thomas Nelson Australia Pty Ltd
19-39 Jeffcott Street West Melbourne
Victoria 3003

Nelson Canada Ltd
81 Curlew Drive Don Mills Ontario M3A 2R1

Thomas Nelson (Nigeria) Ltd
8 Ilupeju Bypass PMB 2 1303 Ikeja Lagos

ISBN 0 17 566185 5
NCN 6624 50 3

Printed in Hong Kong

West Indian Cookery

Contents

Introduction

How to Cook Foods

Food is cooked for the following reasons:

1 To make it more appetizing or tasty e.g. meat, fish, eggs
2 To soften it and make it more digestible e.g. potatoes
3 To extract nourishment from pieces too hard to eat e.g. bones
4 To purify it e.g. milk
5 To make it keep better

Food can be cooked in the following ways:

boiling	grilling	baking
steaming	stewing	roasting
	frying	

Each of these is dealt with in the chapters that follow.

Measuring

If every dish we cook is to be a success, and if we are anxious to avoid waste due to failures, we must *always* take the trouble to measure properly.

Many people cannot afford weights and scales, and some of the people who have them are too lazy to use them. On the whole the quickest and easiest way to measure is by using cups and spoons. Because cups and spoons are of different sizes, it is wise to buy the special kind sold for measuring.

All measures should be absolutely level. This is because different people have different ideas about what is meant by a heaped spoonful. On the few occasions when you are told to use a heaped spoon, see that there is as much piled up as there is in the spoon itself.

Unless told to take a heaped measure, *always* take a knife and pass it across the top to remove any surplus food.

ABBREVIATIONS

teaspoon	= teasp.
tablespoon	= tbsp.
ounce	= oz.
pound	= lb.
pint	= pt.

EQUIVALENTS
Remember that measures should be level

4 saltsp.	= 1 teasp.
3 teasp.	= 1 tbsp.
16 tbsp.	= 1 cup
1 pint	= 2 brimming glasses or 2 breakfast cups
1 "bottle"	= 1½ pts.
½ "bottle"	= ¾ pt.
1 nip	= ½ pt.

Food	Cups per lb.	Tbsp. per oz.
Flour	4 after sifting	4
Wholewheat	3½ approx.	3½
Cornmeal	3	3
Bran	6¼	5⅓
Rice	2 slightly heaped	2
White sugar	2	2
Brown sugar	3 approx.	3
Icing sugar	3¼	3
Cornstarch	3	3
Cocoa	3½ approx.	3
Raisins } Currants }	2⅖	1½
Butter } Lard }	2	2

N.B.—If a half or a quarter cup of butter is required, put half a cup or three-quarters of a cup of water into the measure, and then add butter until the water reaches the top.

2 *Boiling*

Boiling? Why, we all know how to do that, you say, but just let us make sure you really do.

Boiling is a quick easy way of cooking which makes food easy to digest, but unless the process is carefully carried out it may make food broken, unattractive, and tasteless.

Boiling is generally done for one of two reasons:

1 To soften foods such as ground provisions, ham, etc.
2 To extract nourishment from foods, such as cowheel, etc.

When cooking to soften food leave the food in large pieces, and unless very hard place it in boiling water. Boil it very gently for as short a time as possible, so that it will not break, nor will nourishment be lost. Additional heat which makes the water bubble violently does not raise the temperature of the water nor hasten cooking. Fast cooking is therefore definitely undesirable; it not only breaks the food, but is extravagant because more fuel is used.

When extracting nourishment from food cut it in small pieces to expose as much of the inside as possible. Place it in cold water, heat slowly to boiling-point, and cook for a long time.

In both cases there should be enough water to cover the food.

Recipes for boiled foods

CURRIED RICE
1

½oz. (1 tbsp.) butter or oil
1 medium sized onion
1 medium sized tomato
1 teasp. salt
1 tbsp. curry powder or
massala

8 oz. (1 heaped cup) rice
2¼ cups water (use the
cup used for
measuring rice)

Peel onion, wash tomato, and slice both. Heat oil and
lightly fry onion. Add tomato, salt and massala, and cook
again without browning. Put in water and rice
(previously picked and washed), and boil till rice is soft
and grainy. No water should be left, and care is needed
to see that the rice does not burn.

RICE AND PEAS
2

1 cup split peas
½ teasp. bicarbonate
of soda
1 clove of garlic
8 oz. of soup meat
1 pt. (2 glasses) water
1 oz. fat pork or 1 tbsp.
cooking oil

1 cup rice
1 or 2 blades chive
1 small onion
thyme, parsley, tomato
⅛ teasp. black pepper
or small piece green
pepper
1 teasp. salt

Pick and wash peas, and soak them overnight in water
(about 2 glasses) containing half teasp. bicarbonate of
soda.
Next day wash the soup meat quickly, then cut it up.
Boil peas, soup meat, and garlic in the water in which
the peas were soaking. Omit the soda when using soft

rain water. Boil gently so that the peas are softened without being turned into a soup-like condition.

Peel, wash the seasonings, and cut them up, then brown lightly in the fat pork or oil to develop the flavour. When peas are nearly soft add 2 cups boiling water and all other ingredients. Cook until both rice and peas are soft but grainy.

If liked, the rice may be cooked in a separate pan and added when soft.

3   HAM

To every medium-sized ham allow 1 cup brown sugar and 2 tbsp. vinegar. These improve the flavour.

Thoroughly wash and if necessary scrape the ham. Soak it overnight to draw out excess salt.

Place in a large pan with sugar and vinegar. Cover with cold water and heat quickly to boiling-point. Simmer gently, allowing 20 min. to every lb. of ham and 20 over on the whole piece, e.g. 10 lb. ham—boil for $10 \times 20 + 20$ min. $= 220$ min., or 3 hrs. 40 min. Skim during boiling if necessary.

After removing from the fire, let the ham remain in the water for 30 min., then take it out of the water, and when nearly cold remove the brown skin.

Sprinkle top of ham with golden brown bread or biscuit crumbs.

N.B. Sugar and vinegar may be omitted when boiling good quality hams. The ham skin may be boiled up in stock or soup to give additional flavour.

SOUSE 4

half a pig's head   1 pig's tongue
2 trotters

Scald the meat, then scrape and wash thoroughly,
using lime juice.

Tie meat in a floured cloth, place in a pan of cold water
and simmer slowly till tender, about 1¼ hrs. Cool the
meat in the water in which it was boiled. Skin and slice
the tongue. Slice the meat from the head. Cut open the
trotters.

Place the meat in a deep dish, add 2 teasp. salt, juice of
4 limes, and cold water to cover. Soak overnight. Next
day wash meat, then serve in a good sauce made from
juice of 2 limes, 2 teasp. salt, 1 fresh pepper, half a slice
cucumber, 1 cup stock.

BOILED FOWL 5

1 fowl   1 hard-boiled egg
stuffing (recipe 325)   chopped parsley
1 pt. coating sauce   carrot, turnip, onion
   (recipe 250)

An old fowl can be made tender by careful boiling.

Preparation

Pluck and singe the bird.

Cut skin around the knee joints, twist and remove feet
and lower leg, at the same time drawing out tough
sinews.

Cut off the head, make a slit along the back of the neck
to the body. Loosen the skin, cut off the neck close to
the body, but leave the skin on the bird.

Cut the skin round the vent, then loosen and remove
the internal organs. Remove gall from liver and stones
from gizzard. These parts are called the giblets.

Cut out the oil sack just above the tail.
Thoroughly wash the bird inside and out.
Scald the feet and remove scales and toes.

To truss the fowl for boiling
Put a finger in the neck end and loosen skin round the
legs. Push the legs upward till they slip inside the skin.
Draw the skin smoothly over the bird to make an even
surface for coating it with sauce when cooked. Turn the
wings in under the bird and tie in place. Stuff the bird
and fold the skin over at the neck.

To boil fowl
Rub the breast with lime juice to whiten it. Wrap in
greased paper.
Place it with breast down in boiling water, boil for 3 min.
and skim well.
Add a small onion, piece of carrot and turnip, prepared
giblets and half teasp. salt.
Simmer fowl gently till tender, allowing 2-3 hrs. for an
old bird.
Remove the string, dry the bird, and place on a hot dish.
Coat with sauce—a white sauce is generally used—and
garnish with sieved or chopped hard-boiled egg yolk
and chopped parsley.
N.B. Reserve the liquid in which the fowl was boiled for
soup, gravy, etc.

6   BOILED FISH

a large piece of fish	parsley
salt and vinegar	lime
water	sauce

Scale, wash, and trim the fish. Tie it into shape if
necessary.
Boil enough water to cover the fish, add salt and vinegar
in the proportion of 1 tbsp. salt and half teasp. vinegar or

lime juice to every quart (4 glasses) water.

Put in the fish to simmer very gently till cooked. For a large piece of fish allow 10 min. for every pound and 10 min. over on the whole. For small pieces allow 15-20 min.

When the fish looks white instead of watery, drain well, and place on a hot dish. Decorate with slices of lime. Serve with sauce.

N.B. The vinegar is used to whiten fish. It need not be used when cooking dark oily fish.

EDDOES IN SAUCE　　　　　　　　7

about 1 lb. small white
   (Chinese) eddoes
1 tbsp. butter

2 tbsp. vinegar
juice of $\frac{1}{2}$ lime
red pepper to taste

Wash and boil eddoes in their skins.
Melt butter, add vinegar, lime juice, and pepper.
When eddoes are soft, squeeze (pulp) them from their skins and pour over the sauce.
Serve hot with stewed salt fish or similar food.

PAIMI OR CONKIES　　　　　　　　8

1 lb. cornmeal or grated
   fresh corn ($3\frac{3}{4}$ cups)
2 tbsp. lard
2 tbsp. butter
   or margarine
2 tbsp. raising, if liked
$\frac{1}{2}$ a dried coconut
   ($1\frac{1}{2}$ cups)
$\frac{1}{2}$ cup grated pumpkin

2 teasp. salt
$\frac{1}{4}$ teasp. black
   pepper
8 oz. meat
   (fresh or salt)
about 1 nip (1 glass)
   water
2 bunch banana leaves
cotton to tie

} or 1 cup sugar

Grate coconut and pumpkin. Clean the meat and brown in the lard or butter, then brown the seasonings. Chop or mince meat and add all dry ingredients. Stir in enough water to mix to a firm dough.

Wipe banana leaves and heat them to make them pliable. Cut them into pieces about 6 in. by 6 in. Place about 2 tbsp. of the mixture in each piece of leaf, roll up, fold over, and tie the ends. Place in boiling water and boil for ¾ hr.

9   PASTELLES

Sufficient to make one dozen

4 cornballs or 3 cups grated fresh corn	1 green pepper
1 lb. beef steak	1 tbsp. vinegar
1 lb. pork	1 bunch chives
12 olives, if liked	1 clove garlic
1 small bottle capers } if liked	3 medium-sized tomatoes
4 oz. raisins	1 teasp. salt
4 oz. onions	¼ teasp. black pepper
2 oz. fat pork	2 bunches banana leaves
2 tbsp. lard	Cotton to tie
2 tbsp. butter	

Clean and cut up the meat and prepare all seasonings. Melt the fat pork, add half the lard and all the butter. Brown the meat and seasonings and stew for 15 min. Mince the meat and seasonings, and add all ingredients except corn and lard.

Wipe, heat, and cut the banana leaves into pieces 7 in. by 7 in. Crush the corn, adding salted water if necessary. Grease the leaves and spread corn mixture on them—about ⅛ to ¼ in. thick and 5 in. square.

Add about 2 tbsp. meat mixture. Roll, and fold over the ends of leaves. Place in boiling water and cook 1 hr. from the time it boils.

COO-COO 10

1 cup cornmeal	1 teasp. salt
3 to 4 ochroes	1 tbsp. butter
¾ pt. (1½ nips) water or milk and water	

Wash and slice ochroes, add salt, and boil them in half the liquid. When the ochroes are soft enough to be swizzled, mix the cornmeal with the rest of the liquid. Stir this paste into the boiling liquid and continue to cook, stirring all the time until the mixture is thick and smooth. Turn out into well-buttered mould or basin.

BREADFRUIT COO-COO 11

1 breadfruit	2 teasp. salt
4-8 oz. cooked seasoned meat	about ½ glass (½ nip) water or stock

Boil, peel, and pound the breadfruit. Mince or chop meat and seasonings. Mix all ingredients and re-heat. Stir continuously until all the liquid has boiled away. Shape in a well-buttered basin or mould.

CASSAVA COO-COO 12

2 cups grated and sifted sweet cassava	½ teasp. salt
	½ pt. (1 glass) water

Boil water, add salt, stir in cassava. Cook thoroughly at least 7-10 min., by which time mixture should be stiff. Stir all the time. Turn into a greased bowl and shape. Serve hot.

13   JUG JUG

1 pt. (2 glasses) pigeon
  peas
10 tbsp. or a good ½ cup
  guinea cornflour
4 oz. fresh or salt beef

4 oz. lean pork
1 small onion
2 to 3 blades chive
thyme and parsley
salt and pepper

Clean, cut up, and season the beef and pork. If salt beef is used it should be soaked. Stew the pork for 20 min., then add beef and peas and stew for another half-hour or until peas are soft. Strain off, but reserve the water, and mince or chop meat and peas.

Take ½-pt. (1 glass) of the water in which meat was stewed, add meat and peas, and stir in the cornflour. Cook for 15-30 min., stirring all the time. The mixture should be of the same consistency as coo-coo. Shape in a buttered basin and serve hot.

14   DUMPLINGS

Sufficient for 8 medium dumplings

4 oz. (1 cup) flour
2 tbsp. bread-crumbs,
  if liked
⅛ teasp. salt

2 to 3 tbsp. shortening
  (see footnote, page
  42)
1 teasp. baking powder,
  or ¼ teasp. baking soda

Sift flour, wash and chop suet or fat pork. Mix all dry ingredients and add enough cold water to mix to a stiff dough. Knead lightly, form into balls. Put in boiling water or soup, and cook 30 min.

SEASONED DUMPLINGS 15

1 teasp. chopped onion
1 blade chopped chive
1 teasp. chopped parsley

piece of thyme stripped
from stalk

Add to dumplings before mixing with water.

CORNMEAL DUMPLINGS 16

½ cup flour
½ cup cornmeal
⅛ teasp. salt
½ teasp. baking powder

2 to 3 tbsp. shortening
(see footnote, page
42)

Make in the same way as ordinary dumplings.

CASSAVA DUMPLINGS 17

1 cup grated sweet
    cassava
½ cup flour

½ teasp. baking powder
¼ teasp. salt
water to mix

Mix dry ingredients, add enough cold water to bind.
Knead, shape into balls, and boil 20 min. in soup or
boiling water.
N.B. If bitter cassava is used, squeeze out all juice, then
dry and sift the meal before mixing it with flour.

3 Stewing

This is a favourite way of cooking, but many people only make what they call "Beef Stew," with a Pelau every now and again for a change. This is a pity, because although stewing is a slow way of cooking, it is cheap and can be used for any kind of food.

It is cheap because tough pieces of meat having much skin and bone, old and fibrous vegetables, or hard under-ripe fruit can be softened and made tasty by long slow stewing. There is no waste, as any nourishment drawn out from bones, any mineral salts from vegetables or fruit, are all found in the gravy or syrup. Meat and vegetables can also be stewed together, so that fuel and work are saved.

Stewing must be done very gently and slowly so that all the nourishment can be drawn out of the raw food. Unfortunately this slow cooking destroys all the Vitamin C, and it is therefore important that plenty of raw vegetables (or fruit) are served with a stew.

General rules for stewing

1 Cut food in small pieces in order to expose the inside.
2 Having heated the stew to boiling-point, allow it to simmer (i.e. hardly bubble at all).

3 Use a pot with a cover, or the food will lose its flavour and may dry up.
4 Try to add enough liquid (water, stock, or milk) at the start to last throughout the cooking.

BEEF STEW 18

1 lb. stewing beef, (shin, aitchbone or shoulder)
1 teasp. salt
½ teasp. pepper
seasonings, (chive, onion, thyme, or tomato)

1 teasp. brown sugar
2 tbsp. flour
1 tbsp. vinegar, if liked
3 tbsp. oil or dripping, or 1 tbsp. fat pork and 2 tbsp. oil
1 pt. (2 nips) cold water

Clean the meat thoroughly and cut into neat ½-in. cubes, or joint according to the shape of the bones. Prepare the seasonings, add to the meat, and leave for 20-30 min. Choose a thick saucepan or pot, heat the oil, add the sugar, and cook just until it bubbles. While oil and sugar are heating remove seasonings from the meat, coat with flour, and fry in hot oil in an uncovered pot. This browning improves the appearance and the taste of the stew, and in the case of lean meat, forms a coating on the outside which prevents too much of the meat juice running out. Either draw meat to the side of the pot or remove it altogether, and then brown the seasonings. Mix meat, seasonings, and water; cover, heat to boiling-point, and simmer for 1½-2 hrs.

BEEF AND VEGETABLE STEW 19

To the ingredients used for beef stew, add about:
1½ lb. ground provisions, e.g. potato, carrot, eddo, yam

1 teasp. salt
½ pt. (1 nip) water

20   SALMI D'AGOUTI

1 agouti (about 4 lb. in
   weight)
2 teasp. salt
1 teasp. pepper
2 onions (medium)
2 to 3 blades chive
2 tbsp. rum

4 oz. fat bacon
2 pt. water or stock or
   part stock and part
   white wine
1 tbsp. butter
1 tbsp. vinegar, if liked

Skin, clean, and joint the agouti.
Make the stew in the same way as beef stew, adding
rum and wine (if used) just before serving.

21   PELAU

1 fowl or 1 lb. stewing
   beef and 1½ lb. salt
   beef
2 teasp. salt
1 teasp. black pepper or
   1 green pepper
seasonings, e.g. chive,
   onion, thyme, tomato

a few olives
about 12 to 15 parched
   nuts or almonds
3 tbsp. oil
1 tbsp. butter
2 teasp. sugar
2 pt. (4 nips) cold water
2 cups or 1 lb. rice

Pluck, singe, and joint the fowl or clean and cut up the
beef. Make in the same way as beef stew. Simmer for
1½ hrs., then add the rice previously picked and washed.
Boil until rice is soft. No water should remain, so care
must be taken to prevent burning. Add butter and nuts
roughly chopped. Serve on a hot dish decorated with
olives.

PEPPER POT 22

1 oxtail or fowl or duck,
   or any game in season
3 lb. fresh lean pork
1 lb. pickled pork
4 peppers
1 bunch thyme

1 lb. onions
2 heaped tbsp. brown
   sugar
½ to 1 gill (¼ to ½ glass)
   casseripe

Clean and cut meat into small pieces. Put in a large canaree (casserole) and cover with plenty of water. Cover and simmer for 2 hrs. Add peppers (tied in a net bag), thyme, sliced onions, sugar, and casseripe. Simmer again till meat is tender. Boil up every day to prevent food turning bad. Add fresh meat from time to time (the meat must be unseasoned, and nothing starchy may be put in, or pepper pot will turn sour).

CURRIED BEEF STEW 23

1 lb. beef
1 teasp. salt
¼ teasp. pepper
1 or 2 onions
1 or 2 blades chive
1 tomato
1 tbsp. sultanas or
   raisins, if liked

1 small fruit, e.g. mango,
   golden-apple, etc., to
   thicken
about 1 tbsp. curry (the
   quantity varies with
   the kind)
3 tbsp. oil
1 pt. (2 nips) coconut
   milk or water

Clean, cut up, and season meat. Omit sugar, because curry should not be brown. Lightly fry meat, curry, and seasonings in a covered pot, but do not let them brown. Add sultanas and sliced or chopped fruit and coconut milk. Simmer for 1½ hrs., and serve with rice.
(For dry Indian curry see Chapter 22, Some East Indian Recipes.)

24   CURRIED CRAB

2 large crabs
1 teasp. salt
¼ teasp. pepper
1 onion
1 or 2 blades chive
1 tomato

about ½ tbsp. curry
powder or massala
2 tbsp. oil
1 tbsp. butter
water

Scald crabs and wash very thoroughly. Limb crabs, remove body from shell and throw away the gall which clings to the shell. Lightly fry chopped seasonings in hot oil, curry and cook 5 min. without browning. Put in crabs and enough cold water to make a gravy, about ½ pt. (1 glass). Simmer ¾ hr., add butter, and serve on a hot dish. N.B. If time permits cut open claws, pick out crab meat, and return this to the curry, keeping only one or two claws to decorate the dish.

25   CRAB PELAU

2 large crabs
2 to 3 teasp. salt
½ teasp. pepper
1 to 2 onions
1 to 2 blades
chive
1 tomato

about 1 tbsp. curry
powder or massala
3 tbsp. oil
1 tbsp. butter
1¾ cups (or about ¾ lb.)
rice
3½ cups coconut milk

Make as for curried crab, using coconut milk instead of water. After simmering for ½ hr., by which time the coconut milk should have boiled down to 3 cupfuls, add the rice and cook until it is soft. Add butter, and serve piled up on a hot dish.

CRAB GUMBO 26

6 crabs
3 large tomatoes
1 onion
1 to 2 blades chive
¼ red pepper without
   seeds
water

piece of parsley or
   thyme
1 bay leaf
6 to 7 ochroes
2 tbsp. butter
salt to taste

Purge, scald, and thoroughly wash the crabs. Remove claws and take body from shell, discarding the gall. Cut body into four. Scald and skin tomatoes, if liked. Wash and cut up seasonings and slice ochroes. Melt butter and brown crabs. Add seasonings, and when brown put in ochroes. When all are well browned add bay leaf and enough water to cover—about 2-2½ pt. Cover pot and simmer 1 hr. When cooked mixture should be like thick soup. Serve in a hot tureen with rice.

CURRIED SHRIMPS 27

1 lb. shrimps—about 2
   large handfuls
1 teasp. salt
¼ teasp. pepper
seasonings—onion,
   chive, tomato

about 1 tbsp. curry or
   massala
2 tbsp. oil
1 tbsp. butter
water

Scald shrimps, shell, cut open along the back, and remove black cord. Wash well with lime juice. Lightly fry seasonings (use a covered pot to prevent browning), add curry, and cook 5 min. Put in shrimps and enough cold water to make a gravy (about 1 cupful). Simmer till shrimps are soft—about 15-20 min. Add butter, serve on a hot dish with a border of rice. Decorate with pieces of red pepper.

N.B. If no gravy is required, add only about 2-3 tbsp. of water, cover closely, and allow shrimps to steam rather than stew. Use a low heat.

28 STEWED TURTLE

2 lb. turtle	1 tbsp. vinegar or lime juice
1 teasp. salt	
2 to 3 blades chive	½ teasp. ground spice and clove
1 medium-sized onion	
2 tbsp. brandy	3 tbsp. olive oil or cooking oil
1 glass sherry or dry white wine	
pepper	2 tbsp. butter
2 medium-sized tomatoes	1 tbsp. sugar

Boil bay leaves in 1½ pt. water. Pour liquid over turtle and soak for 10 min. Clean and wash turtle in this water. Sprinkle with vinegar or lime juice and season with salt, pepper, chive, tomatoes, onion, spice and clove, brandy, and wine. Allow to stand for 15 min. Heat oil and butter, brown the sugar, add meat without seasonings, and cook for about 45 min. on slow fire. Then add all seasonings, and allow to simmer gently till turtle is soft.

N.B. If more gravy is needed add more wine or some stock.

STEWED FISH 29

Suitable for young children or invalids

1 lb. fish—sliced or if
    possible boned
1 teasp. salt
½ teasp. pepper
1 or 2 blades chive
1 onion—small

1 teasp. chopped parsley
1 blade mace
2 tbsp. butter
1 pt. (1 glass) water
1 tbsp. flour
a little milk

Clean and cut fish in slices or cutlets. Season for not
more than 20 min. Fry fish and seasonings very lightly in
a covered aluminium or enamel-lined saucepan. Add
water and simmer gently for about 20 min. Mix flour to a
paste with a little cold milk and stir this in to thicken the
gravy. Add parsley and boil again for 5 min., stirring all
the time. Serve on a hot dish decorated with sliced
tomato.

CURRIED FISH 30

Cook in the same way as stewed fish, adding about 1
tbsp. curry to the fish and seasonings. If possible, use
coconut milk instead of water. Leave out the cow's
milk, mace, and parsley.

STEWED SALT FISH 31

½ lb. salt fish
2 tomatoes
chive, onion, and pepper
    to taste
1 tbsp. cooking oil
1 tbsp. butter

1 tbsp. flour
about ¾ pt. (1½ glasses)
    water
about ¼ teasp. roocoo to
    colour, if liked

Scald salt fish, remove skin and bone, and cut into 1-1½ in. pieces. Heat oil and butter and lightly fry seasonings. Stir in the flour, then add fish and enough water to make a good sauce. Cover and stew until fish is tender, about 20 min.

32 STEWED CASCADURA

6 medium-sized cascadura	2 medium-sized onions
1 bunch chive	1½ teasp. salt
3-4 medium-sized tomatoes	pepper
½ teasp. ground spice and clove	3 tbsp. oil
	2 tbsp. butter
	1 whole lime
2 teasp. vinegar or lime juice	1 tbsp. sugar
	¾ pt. (1½ nips) water

Put cascadura in a pail of water and rub from head to tail with a piece of cloth to remove mud. Rub with lime and salt to get rid of slime. Clean and season in the usual way. Heat oil and brown the sugar till bubbly. Brown cascadura in an uncovered pot (about 10-15 min.). Add seasonings, and when brown put in the water. Simmer till fish is cooked (about 20-30 min.).

33 SALT FISH IN CHEMISE

½ lb. salt fish	1 small tomato
2 tbsp. oil	thyme
¼ teasp. pepper	2 eggs
1 or 2 blades chive	½ tbsp. flour
½ onion	½ pt. (1 nip) water

Scald salt fish, remove skin and bone, and flake finely. Heat oil and lightly fry seasonings without browning. Add flour and water, then fish, and simmer for 10 min.

Place the mixture in a greased fire-proof dish (e.g. enamel or Pyrex), and break the eggs over it. Bake or steam until the eggs set. Serve at once.

PIGEON PEA STEW 34

2 cups shelled peas	seasonings—chive,
6 to 8 oz. salt beef	onion, tomato, thyme,
½ lb. pumpkin	garlic
2 pot-spoons cooking oil	½ teasp. pepper

Soak salt beef for at least ½ hr., and then cut it into ½-in. pieces. Shell peas; peel, wash, and chop pumpkin; pound garlic; chip seasonings. Lightly fry seasonings, pumpkin, and peas in a covered pot. Add meat and water, and simmer for 1 hr. When cooked the pumpkin should be mashed, and the peas must be soft but whole.

CURRIED BREADNUTS (Chataigne) 35

1 full (but not ripe) breadnut	2 tbsp. butter or fat pork
2 dried coconuts	1 teasp. salt
1 tbsp. curry	seasonings—onion, chive, thyme, tomato

Peel chataigne and divide into natural divisions. Boil for 2 hrs. then squeeze dry. Take out and peel seeds. Prepare and lightly fry the seasonings, add the curry powder, flesh and nuts from the chataigne. Make and add about 1 pt. (2 glasses) coconut milk, and stew till nuts are soft. Serve on a hot dish with a border of rice and a border of grated coconut. Decorate with pieces of fried salt fish.

36 STEWED FRUIT

1 lb. fruit (full but not ripe   ½ pt. (1 nip) water
    golden apples,   ¾ cup sugar
    pomerac, mammy
    apple, etc.)

Put sugar and water in an aluminium or enamelled
saucepan and boil it without a cover for 10 min.
Meanwhile wash, peel, and cut fruit into neat pieces.
Put fruit in the syrup and simmer very gently till soft, the
time varies with the kind of fruit. When cooked the
pieces of fruit should still be whole and not a broken
mash.

N.B. This is a good way of using up under-ripe fruit which
has fallen from the tree. It is served as a sweet or
dessert, and should not be confused with jam or
conserve.

37 STEWED DRIED FRUIT

Wash, then soak the fruit overnight. Cook in the same
way as fresh fruit.

Soup

4

Most of us know and probably like pea or "pease" soup and sancoche. These and most other well made soups are economical, and in many cases, a nourishing form of food.

Rules for soup making

1 Use an enamelled or aluminium saucepan. Iron pots discolour soup.
2 Except for clear soups, which must be absolutely free from grease, lightly fry all seasonings and vegetables. This frying, or sautéing, as it is sometimes called, develops the flavour. It must be done without browning the food, so that a covered pan is often used.
3 Carefully distinguish between sieving and straining. When sieving soup, everything except bones, hard seeds or skins, etc., must be pressed through the sieve. When straining, no crushing of vegetables or seasonings should be done.
4 Always put bones or soup meat in cold water and cook for a long time. The foundation of most good soup is well-made stock—that is, the water in which meat or fish and vegetables have been boiled. People who have a refrigerator should make stock overnight.

38   FIRST OR BEST STOCK

2 lb. shin of beef for brown stock *or* 2 lb. knuckle of veal or cow-heel for white stock	2 qt. (8 nips) cold water 1 carrot and onion or other seasoning 1 sprig parsley and thyme 1 teasp. salt

Wipe or wash the meat, cut into small pieces and remove all fat. Chop the bones, if necessary, and remove any marrow which is fatty. Put meat, salt, and water in a large saucepan. Cover and heat slowly to boiling-point. Skim well and add seasonings whole or cut in large pieces not slices, because stock must not be made cloudy. Simmer for 3-4 hrs. to extract all nourishment, then strain into a basin which should stand on a wire grid or sieve so that air can pass underneath. When cold, stock should be in jelly form. Remove fat that has risen to the top and reserve it for frying, roasting, etc.

39   SECOND OR HOUSEHOLD STOCK

scraps of cooked meat cooked or uncooked bones vegetables	clear gravy salt water

Make in the same way as first stock. Avoid using any greasy or starchy scraps for the stock.

Broths

CREOLE PEA SOUP 40
Serves 6

1 lb. soup meat or salt
  beef
2 tbsp. oil or butter
½ cup split peas
2 pt. (4 nips) water
1 lb. root vegetables
  (5 medium size)

2 teasp. salt (less if salt
  beef)
¼ teasp. black pepper
small pinch baking soda
2 to 3 blades chive
1 onion

Pick, wash, and soak peas overnight. Wash and cut up seasonings and meat (soak salt meat for ½ hr. before cutting up). Heat oil till smoking, lightly fry seasonings and set on one side. Brown any lean meat but not bone or salt beef. Put water, meat, peas, and soda to cook in a covered pot. When boiling skim well and add prepared seasonings. Simmer till peas are thoroughly softened —about 1 hr.—and mash if necessary. Peel and wash root vegetables, cut into neat slices or dice, add to the soup with salt and cook till soft—about 30 min. Add dumplings, if liked (see recipe 14). Serve very hot.

SANCOCHE 41
Serves 4-6

¾ lb. pickled meat,
  e.g. thick slice salt
  beef, thick slice salt
  pork, pickled pig's tail
1 tbsp. butter or oil
1 qt. (4 nips) water
about 1½ lb. provisions,
  e.g. plantain, tannia,
  sweet potato, green

figs, cassava, pumpkin,
  ochroes, kallaloo
seasonings to taste
½ teasp. salt
¼ teasp. pepper
dumplings, if liked
  (see Recipe 14)

Soak and cut up meat. Peel and cut vegetables into blocks or thick slices. Peel, cut up, and lightly fry seasonings in the butter. Mix all ingredients and simmer till soft—about 1 hr.

42   COW-HEEL SOUP

1 cow-heel	1 tbsp. sago
3 pt. (6 glasses) water	1 teasp. chopped parsley
1 onion	lime juice
1 strip celery	2 teasp. salt
1 carrot	piece of red pepper
1 lb. mixed vegetables	grated nutmeg

Scald, scrape, and thoroughly clean cow-heel. Cut it up and put to boil in salted water. Skim and add chopped seasonings. Simmer gently for 6-7 hrs. Peel, wash, and cut vegetables into dice. Remove meat from bone, cut into neat pieces, and return to soup with prepared vegetables and sago. Boil soup again till vegetables are soft—about 30 min. Add parsley, few drops lime juice, and grated nutmeg just before serving.

43   MUTTON BROTH WITH YOUNG CORN
Serves 6

¾ lb. scrag end of mutton	2 teasp. salt
2 pt. (4 nips) water	onion, chive, parsley,
2 to 3 ears of corn	and pepper

Clean and joint mutton, removing excess fat. Put mutton in cold salted water, heat to boiling-point. Skim, add seasonings, and simmer about 1 hr. Remove covering from corn, wash, and add to soup. Cook till corn is soft—about ½ hr.

FISH BROTH 44

1 fish or fish head—
  about ¾ lb.
1 qt. (4 nips) cold water
1 onion
2 tbsp. butter
3 to 4 Irish potatoes

1½ teasp. salt
¼ teasp. pepper
seasonings, including a
  clove and a blade of
  chive

Cut up seasonings and fry lightly in the butter or pork fat—avoid browning; use a cover if necessary. Clean and add fish, water, and salt. Heat to boiling-point. Skim and add potatoes previously peeled, washed, and diced. Simmer 30-40 min. till soft. Remove fish, separate flesh from skin and bone and return it to the soup. If liked, thicken with 2 tbsp. flour mixed to a smooth paste with ½ nip milk. Boil this paste in the soup 5 min. Garnish with chopped parsley.

CASSAVA BROTH WITH SHRIMPS 45

Sufficient for about 4 people

1 lb. bones
¼ lb. mixed pickled meat
  (e.g. salt beef, pig's
  tail)
a few shrimps

1 green pepper
1 tomato and onion
thyme
2 to 3 sticks cassava
2 pt. (4 nips) water

Wash and simmer bones for 1½ hrs. Clean and cut up meat; peel and wash cassava. Add meat and cassava to stock. Simmer till cassava is soft, then remove and pound it. Scald shrimps and remove shell and the cord down centre back. Prepare seasonings and lightly fry them with shrimps. Add seasonings, shrimps, and cassava to soup and boil till thick. Serve with foo-foo (pounded plantain).

N.B. Fried salt fish may be used in place of shrimps.

46   KALLALOO

1 doz. eddo or dasheen
   leaves
seasonings (including
   garlic) to taste
¼ lb. pickled meat (e.g.
   salt beef) or a ham
   bone

8 ochroes
2 to 3 crabs
1 tbsp. butter
1 pt. boiling water

Soak and cut up salt beef. Scald crabs and scrub well.
Strip the stalks and midrib from leaves, wash and roll
them. Wash and cut up ochroes and seasonings. Put all
ingredients except butter in enamelled or aluminium
saucepan. Pour on boiling water (this makes leaves a
better colour than cold water), and simmer until
everything is soft—about ½–¾ hr. Stir thoroughly, add
butter, and serve when the whole is soft and well
divided. If liked, remove crabs, pick out and return flesh
to the kallaloo before serving. This makes it easier to
eat, but it is not a popular arrangement with most West
Indians! Serve with foo-foo (pounded plantain), see
recipe 324.

47   CHIP-CHIP SOUP

½ pailful chip-chips
about 3 pt. (6 glasses)
   water
2 tannias or other
   vegetables to thicken
1 onion
2 to 3 blades chive

2 teasp. salt
piece red pepper
2 tbsp. butter
1 tbsp. Worcester or
   tomato sauce
lime juice to taste

Wash chip-chips in running water to remove all traces
of sand. Wash again with lime juice. Scald them by
pouring boiling water over them. Put chip-chips in clean

cold water, heat to boiling-point, and cook 10-15 min.
Strain off but reserve this water and to it add prepared
seasonings and peeled sliced tannias. Cook until
tannias can be mashed to thicken the soup. Meanwhile
shake chip-chips in a tray or sieve and remove all shells.
Add butter, chip-chips, and sauce to soup and re-heat.
Avoid overcooking chip-chips or they will be tough.

Cream soups or purées

TANNIA CREAM SOUP   **48**
Serves 4

1 lb. tannias	1 teasp. salt
1 pt. (2 nips) water or	small piece green
light stock	pepper or unground
1 onion	black pepper
1 or 2 blades chive	¼ pt. (½ cup) milk
2 tbsp. butter or oil	about 4 tbsp. fried dice
	of bread (croûtons)

Peel, wash, and roughly cut up tannias and seasonings. Melt butter in an enamelled or aluminium pan and lightly fry tannia and seasonings without browning (use a cover). Add stock and salt; heat to boiling-point, skim, then simmer till tannia is soft and broken down. Rub the mixture through a fine sieve, pouring only a little at a time. Add milk, re-heat and serve at once. Serve with fried croûtons.

49 POTATO CREAM SOUP

Make in the same way as Tannia Cream Soup (recipe 48), using Irish potatoes instead of tannia. Flavour with a blade of mace.

50 EDDO SOUP

Make as for Tannia Soup (recipe 48).
N.B. Any ground provision may be substituted.

51 TOMATO SOUP
Serves 6

1 lb. tomatoes or 1
   medium-sized tin
1 pt. (2 nips) water or
   light stock
1 oz. ham chips—
   cooked or raw
1 teasp. salt
piece of carrot, turnip,
   and onion
sprigs of parsley and
   thyme
grated nutmeg

blade of mace
piece of green pepper or
   5-6 unground black
   peppers
1 tbsp. butter
1 tbsp. starchy food for
   thickening e.g. flour,
   cornstarch, sago, or
   crushed tapioca
½ cup milk, if liked
a little sugar, if liked

Wash and roughly cut up tomatoes and seasonings, except for parsley, thyme, and mace, which should be left whole. Cut up ham and heat slowly to melt any fat. Add butter, then lightly fry seasonings and tomatoes without browning (use a cover). Add stock, herbs, and salt, and simmer until tomatoes are thoroughly soft—about $\frac{1}{2}$-$\frac{3}{4}$ hr. Rub through a fine sieve. Mix cornstarch or flour to a smooth paste with cold water, add to soup, and boil for 5 min. When sago or tapioca is used instead, sprinkle it straight into boiling soup and boil 5 min. If milk is used, add it to the soup at the last and warm without boiling, otherwise the acidity of tomatoes will make it curdle. Finally, season to taste with a little nutmeg and sugar, and if necessary add red colouring, e.g. roocoo. Serve with fried croûtons.

PUMPKIN CREAM SOUP 52
Serves 4

1 lb. pumpkin	grated nutmeg, if liked
1 tomato	1 teasp. salt
piece of carrot, turnip, and onion	2 tbsp. butter or 1 tbsp. butter and a piece of bacon or ham
sprigs of parsley and thyme	1 pt. (2 nips) water or light stock
1 bay leaf	
piece of green pepper or about	1 tbsp. flour or cornstarch
5 whole black peppers	$\frac{1}{4}$ pt. ($\frac{1}{2}$ cup) milk

Make in the same way as Tomato Soup (recipe 51). Mix flour to a paste with milk and boil 5 min.

53   LENTIL SOUP

½ lb. (1 cup) lentils
2 pt. (4 nips) water or
    stock
1 onion
1 bunch soup seasoning
1 bunch herbs
1 green pepper

1 potato to thicken
1 tbsp. butter or dripping
    or a piece of fat pork
1 teasp. salt
¼ pt. (½ cup) milk
dice of fried bread
    (croûtons)

Pick, wash, and soak lentils overnight. Peel, wash, and
cut up vegetables and all seasonings except herbs.
Heat butter and lightly fry vegetables (including lentils)
and seasonings. Avoid browning. Add stock, salt, and
herbs, and simmer till tender—about 1 hr. Stir well or
rub soup through a wire sieve. Re-heat, add milk, and
serve hot.

N.B. Any legumes (e.g. fresh pigeon peas, split peas, red
beans), can be used in place of lentils. If pigeon peas are
used, double the quantity and leave out the soaking.

54   SPINACH SOUP

2 bundles (about 6 oz.)
    spinach
1 large Irish potato
1 large onion
1 teasp. salt
¼ teasp. pepper

1 pt. (2 glasses) water or
    light stock
1 tbsp. butter
1 tbsp. flour
½ pt. (1 glass) milk

Peel, wash, and cut up potato and onion, and put to boil
with water and salt. Wash and strip spinach, and steam
or scald it. Chop finely. Crush or sieve potato and onion,
return to water in which it cooked and add spinach and
butter. Mix flour with a little of the milk, add to soup with
remainder of the milk. Stir and boil 5 min.

WATERCRESS SOUP   55

Use 2 large bundles cress. Wash in several changes of
water and discard all stalks. Make in the same way as
spinach soup.

AVOCADO PEAR SOUP   56

1 tbsp. flour	½ a large pear
1 tbsp. butter	1 teasp. salt
¼ pt. (½ cup) milk	piece of green pepper
1 pt. (2 glasses) white stock	dash of Worcester sauce, if liked

Melt butter, stir in flour without browning. Add milk
gradually, and cook mixture until like a thick white
sauce. Stir in the stock. Just before serving stir in the
pear, previously peeled, and either pounded or sieved.
Warm soup for a few minutes, but avoid boiling, which
causes a bitter taste. Season, strain, and serve at once.

CORN SOUP   57
Serves 6

8-10 fresh corn cobs	1 teasp. salt
1½ pt. (6 nips) white stock	5-6 whole black peppers
½ pt. (1 glass) milk	pinch of sugar, if liked
1 tbsp. butter	

Wash and grate the corn. Lightly fry it in the butter
without browning. Add stock and simmer till corn is
soft—about ½-¾ hr. Sieve soup, re-heat, and add milk.

58 GROUND-NUT SOUP

1 lb. ground-nuts
  (peanuts)
1 pt. (2 glasses) white or
  light stock
1 onion

¼ oz. (½ tbsp.) butter
¼ pt. (½ glass) milk
¾ teasp. salt
piece of red pepper

Parch the nuts, remove shell and brown skins, then mince or pound them finely. Peel and slice onion, and fry it in the butter without browning (use a cover). Add nuts, pepper, salt, and stock. Simmer for about 3 hrs. Skim off oil which forms from nuts and remove pepper. Rub through a sieve. Add milk and re-heat without boiling. gserve with fried dice of bread.

59 BREADNUT SOUP

1 pt. (2 glasses) bread-
  nuts
1 pt. (2 glasses) water or
  light stock
1½ pt. (3 glasses) milk

½ tbsp. sugar
½ oz. (1 tbsp.) butter
¼ oz. (1 tbsp.) flour
squeeze of lime juice
pepper and salt to taste

Boil breadnuts about 15 min. in salted water, then peel and chop them. Melt butter in a white lined pan, add nuts and fry lightly without browning (use a cover). Add sugar, salt, lime juice, and water, and simmer 1 hr. or until nuts are tender. Sieve, add flour mixed to a paste with the milk, and boil again for 10 min. Serve with fried or toasted cubes of bread.

Clear and strained soups

CONSOMMÉ JULIENNE   60

1 qt. (4 nips) best quality stock free from all fat	small bunch of herbs (parsley and thyme)
¼ lb. lean beef	6 black peppers
1 egg white and shell	unground or 1 green
1 small carrot, turnip, and onion	pepper
2 cloves	small blade mace

Clean, chop or mince meat finely, soak in cold stock for
½hr. Peel and cut vegetables into large pieces. Mix all
ingredients, heat to boiling-point, whisking meanwhile.
When mixture has risen almost to the top of the
saucepan, stop whisking, cover and allow soup to
simmer 20-30 min. Strain 2 or 3 times through a cloth.
Re-heat, add 1 tbsp. sherry and serve with suitable
garnish, such as shreds of vegetable previously cooked.

CONSOMMÉ ROYALE   61

Make in the same way as Consommé Julienne (recipe
60), but garnish with small pieces of savoury custard cut
in fancy shapes.

CONSOMMÉ À LA CELESTINE   62

Make in the same way as Consommé Julienne (recipe
60), but garnish with shreds of savoury pancake.

63 CREOLE TURTLE SOUP

½ lb. turtle fin
2 qt. (8 glasses) water
Piece of mace and bay
   leaf
2 onions
2 or 3 blades chive

2-3 whole black peppers
   or piece of red pepper
Clove, garlic, thyme,
   parsley, tomato,
   sherry, if liked

Wash and scald turtle and remove any skin or shell. Cut up, add water and simmer for about 3 hrs. Add seasoning (left whole) and simmer for another hour. Strain soup and add sherry to taste. Garnish with small squares of fin before serving.

N.B. Some people think that the flavour is improved if the turtle is lightly browned in a little hot oil or butter before being simmered. This must be done after scalding.

Steaming 5

Steaming can be done in three ways:
1 Using a proper steamer, which is a metal pan fitting over a saucepan. Sometimes these steamers have a perforated bottom like a strainer to that steam can rise through the holes to cook the food, sometimes they have a tube up the side to carry steam.
2 By putting food in a basin, jug, or carrier, and standing this in a pan half-filled with boiling water.
3 Using a covered plate over a pan of boiling water.

Steaming is a good way of cooking, because when food is cooked in steam instead of being boiled it is much less likely to break, and very little of the nourishment is drawn out; steamed vegetables therefore contain more mineral salts than boiled ones. Since steamed food such as fish is more or less cooked in its own juice, without the addition of water and with little fat, it is very easily digested, so that it is good for people recovering from sickness and for young children, etc. Steaming is also economical, as two or three foods can be cooked over one ring. For example, we might put provisions to boil in a saucepan, spinach in a steamer over them, and fish on a plate on top of that.

Unfortunately steaming is a very slow way of cooking. On this account it can only be used for soft or small pieces of food. It is well suited to the cooking of pumpkin, spinach, googe, cristophine, slices of fish, sweet-bread, custard, etc. Some people have an idea that steamed food is somewhat tasteless and unattractive in appearance. These disadvantages can easily be overcome by careful seasoning and by covering the food with a thick sauce or by garnishing.

Rules for steaming

1   Allow about 1½ times to twice as long as for boiling, e.g. boil a large quantity of rice for 20 min.; steam the same quantity for 40 min.
2   Use half as much salt for steaming as for boiling.
3   Boil the water in the saucepan fast, this makes more steam.
4   Use a pan with a tightly fitting cover to prevent escape of steam.

64   STEAMED PUMPKIN, CABBAGE, SPINACH, OR OTHER GREEN VEGETABLE

Choose only young vegetables.
Remove all uneatable parts and wash the vegetables in the usual way. Cut up if necessary. Place in a steamer, spri rkle a small quantity of salt between each layer, and steam till the toughest part (e.g. stalks) are soft—about 30 min. for a small quantity.

65   STEAMED RICE

2 cups rice   1 teasp. salt   3½ cups water
(N.B. Measure water with the same cup)

Pick and wash rice in the usual way. Put rice, water, and salt in a large enamel jug or other heat-resisting receptacle. Place this in fast boiling water, being careful that the water is not more than two-thirds up the outside of jug, otherwise it may bubble over into the rice water. Steam 30 min., or rather longer for a large

quantity. (This method is often used by the Chinese.)
N.B. The boiling water round the jug should be used for
cooking root vegetables or some other food.

STEAMED CUSTARD 66

1 pt. (2 nips) milk	2-3 tbsp. sugar
2-3 eggs	$\frac{1}{2}$ teasp. essence or spice

Grease a pie-dish or enamelled basin. Lightly beat eggs
(they need not be frothy) with sugar, and add milk and
flavouring. Pour into pie-dish and cover with greased
paper to keep out steam. Place in a steamer or large pot
containing a little boiling water. The piedish should not
rest on the bottom of the pot as this may make the
custard cook too fast, and if it boils at all it will
immediately curdle. For this reason, place two or three
pieces of clean wood or an upturned saucer in the pot
on which to stand the pie-dish. Cover the saucepan and
steam gently for about 1 hr. or until custard sets. The
top may be browned under a grill for the last 15 min.

CABINET PUDDING 67

3 sponge cakes or	1 tbsp. currants or
3 slices stale bread	cherries citron, if liked

CUSTARD

1 nip ($\frac{1}{2}$ pt.) milk	1 tbsp. sugar
2 eggs	$\frac{1}{4}$ teasp. essence or spice

Remove crusts from bread and cut bread or cake into
neat squares. Wash and pick currants and chop citron.
Prepare custard as for Steamed Custard, and mix all
ingredients in a buttered pie-dish or bowl. Stand until
bread is thoroughly soaked, then steam as for Custard
(recipe 66). Serve hot or cold. If served cold it may be
turned out.

68   STEAMED PINEAPPLE PUDDING

2-4 oz. ($\frac{1}{4}$-$\frac{1}{2}$ cup)
  shortening *

4 oz. ($\frac{1}{2}$ cup) sugar

4 oz. (1 cup) flour

2 eggs

2-3 tbsp. diced
  pineapple

1 tbsp. pineapple juice

$\frac{1}{2}$teasp. baking powder

Grease a pudding basin or mould and dredge with flour.
Decorate bottom of basin with pieces of pineapple.
Cream (beat) butter and sugar together till white and
frothy. Whisk eggs, and gradually beat them into the
mixture. Sift and lightly stir in the flour, about one-third
at a time. Add baking powder with last spoonful of flour
and stir in the rest of the pineapple and the juice. See
that the mixture is soft enough to drop from the
spoon—if too stiff add a little milk—and pour into
prepared mould, which should not be more than two-
thirds full. Cover closely with greased paper. Steam 1$\frac{1}{2}$
hrs. and serve hot.

69   PATRIOTIC PUDDING

4 oz. (1 cup) flour

2 oz. (4 tbsp.) shortening

2 oz. (4 tbsp.) sugar

1 egg

$\frac{1}{4}$ cup milk

1 teasp. baking powder

2 tbsp. golden syrup or
  molasses

1 teasp. grated orange
  rind or other flavouring

pinch of salt

Grease a pudding basin or mould and a piece of
greaseproof paper large enough to cover the top of it.
Put the molasses in the bottom of the basin. Wash, dry,

* *Shortening* is another word for grease, such as lard, butter, cooking
oil, suet etc. The kind used will depend on the flavour required, and
whether the pudding is to be sweet or savoury. See also pages 81-82.

and grate the orange, being careful to use the coloured
skin only and none of the bitter white pith. Sift flour and
salt into a mixing bowl and, using finger tips or a fork,
rub in shortening till it looks like fine crumbs. Add sugar,
orange rind, and baking powder and mix well. Beat egg
and add milk, and stir these into dry ingredients. Pour
mixture into prepared basin, which should not be more
than two-thirds full. Cover closely with greased paper.
Steam 2 hr. Turn out and serve hot.

STEAMED FISH   70

2 or 3 slices king fish or grouper, or 1 small red fish	salt and pepper
	lime juice
	1 tbsp. butter
seasonings to taste	

Clean and season fish in the usual way.
Prepare a pan of boiling water and butter a plate or
carrier. Put fish with its seasoning in prepared plate or
carrier, with a small dab of butter on each piece. Add
lime juice, cover closely and steam. Allow 25 min. for
small slices of fish; or 15 min. to each pound and 15
min. more if steaming a large fish. Use the liquid which
collects round the fish to make a creole or white sauce.
Garnish with slices of lime or tomato.

STEAMED CHICKEN   71

See Chinese Dishes, Chapter 23.

6 Frying

Fried food is very tasty but too much of it can cause indigestion. In order to make fried food tasty and attractive in appearance the oil or fat must be made very hot, and this great heat changes oil into an indigestible form. For this reason it is unwise to give fried food to young children, invalids, or anyone with a weak digestion, and even healthy people should eat it only occasionally.

Kinds of frying

1 Shallow frying
Used for cooking small or thin pieces of food such as pancakes, bacon rashers, eggs, and sometimes fish and meat. Use just enough oil to prevent the food from sticking, or for fish, etc., take enough to reach half-way up the piece of food.

2 Deep frying
Use enough oil to cover the food completely. Because of this the food cooks more quickly, and no turning is necessary, so that food browns more evenly and is less likely to break. Some people imagine that the use of so much oil is extravagant, but provided that care is taken to prevent the oil from burning, it can be used over and over again. Deep frying should be used rather than shallow frying whenever cooking large quantities or large pieces of food.

Kinds of fat for frying

Butter
This gives food a delicious flavour, but it is expensive and burns very easily. It should only be used for frying omelettes or very small pieces of food.

Margarine
This is sometimes used instead of butter, but does not give as good a flavour.

Lard
Some people object to lard on the ground that it makes food greasy. This does not happen if the lard is hot enough when food is put in.

Dripping (from a roast)
Can be used after the gravy which collects at the bottom has been removed.

Fat pork
Can be used when frying small quantities of food. It should first be washed, cut into small pieces, and then heated very gradually to melt out the oil from the skin. It is often mixed with other fat to improve the flavour.

Edible oil
Gives excellent results and is best when frying large quantities. Some people find that lard gives a better flavour.

TO MAKE OIL OR DRIPPING
from large pieces of meat fat or suet

Wash fat, remove any lean or pieces of thick skin. Cut into small pieces, cover with cold water and simmer until all the fat has melted. Strain into a basin; cool and then skim off the fat and throw away the water.

TO MAKE COCONUT OIL

2 very dry coconuts
about ¼ pt. of water (½ nip)

this gives about
¼ pt. of oil

1st method

Grate coconuts, add water and knead for about 5 min. to work out milk. Strain. Boil milk without stirring till it turns to oil—1-1½ hrs. Strain, cool, and bottle.

2nd method

Prepare coconut milk as above. Strain, and add 1 to 1½ teasp. lime juice and a pinch of salt. Stand for 12 hrs., by which time oil separates from water and floats at the top. Skim off the oil and boil for 20-30 min., until all water has been dried off. Strain, cool, and bottle.

TO CLARIFY (OR CLEAN) OIL WHICH HAS BEEN BURNED

Allow the oil to cool, add about three times as much water as there is oil, and boil the two together for about 15 min. Pour into a basin, cool, skim off the fat, and throw away the water.

General rules for frying

1 Use an iron or steel frying pan or pot. Enamel frying pans crack very quickly with the great heat of the oil, and aluminium pans, which must not be washed with soda, are a nuisance to clean after frying.
2 Use a deep pot for deep frying.
3 Always see that the oil is smoking before putting in any food. Bubbling or boiling does not mean that oil is hot enough for frying, only that there is water or gravy in it. The smoke should be in the form of a faint

blue vapour—not a dark brownish smoke, which means that the oil is overheated.

4 Do not put too much food into the oil at once; this cools the oil and is as bad as starting with cold oil. If the oil is not hot enough the food breaks, and becomes sodden and very indigestible.

5 Dry food before frying it. If wet pieces of fish or wet potato chips, etc., are put into the oil they make it cold, and sometimes make it bubble so much that it boils over.

6 Coat any protein foods, except eggs, before frying. This dries them, makes them brown more easily, and helps to form a crisp outside which will keep in any nourishment. The following coatings may be used:

Dry flour—a quick coating for meat, fish, ripe plantain, etc.

Bread-crumbs (fresh)	Used with a thin paste of flour and water or beaten egg, which makes the breadcrumbs, etc., stick. These are good coatings for meat or fish cutlets, beef balls, rissoles, etc.
Raspings (dried bread-crumbs)	
Farine	
Crushed vermicelli	
Oatmeal	

7 Drain fried foods thoroughly. All foods except meat and eggs should be drained on a piece of clean crumpled absorbent paper.

8 Do not cover fried foods closely while hot. This will make them lose their crispness.

9 Strain any surplus oil after frying is finished. If pieces of meat or fish are left in it, they will go bad and spoil the oil.

10 Wipe greasy pans or pots with kitchen paper before washing—they will then be easier to clean.

72   FRIED MELONGENE

Peel, wash, and cut melongene into lengths $\frac{1}{4}$ to $\frac{1}{2}$ in.
thick. Sprinkle with salt, white pepper, and finely
chopped chive (if liked). Allow to stand for 5-10 min.,
remove chive and fry in hot smoking oil. Sprinkle with
powdered bread-crumbs or raspings and serve hot.

73   FRIED OCHROE

Wash ochroes, cut off stem and cut into four
lengthways. Season with salt and pepper, roll in dry
flour, and fry in smoking hot oil:

74   FRIED BREADFRUIT

If breadfruit is almost ripe, peel, wash, cut into six or
eight slices, remove core, and treat in the same manner
as Melongene. If breadfruit is green, boil or steam
before frying.

75   FRIED POTATO CHIPS

Peel, wash, and cut potatoes into $\frac{1}{4}$ to $\frac{1}{2}$ in. slices. Cut
into $\frac{1}{4}$ to $\frac{1}{2}$ in. strips, and soak in salt water for about 20-
30 min. Dry thoroughly, and fry in smoking hot oil till
golden brown and crisp outside and soft in the middle.

76   BAKES

$\frac{1}{2}$ lb. (2 cups) flour	2 teasp. baking powder
1 oz. (2 tbsp.) shortening	or 1 teasp.
1 teasp. salt	bicarbonate of soda
2 teasp. sugar	

Sift flour, salt, and baking powder together. Add the
shortening, and using finger tips or a fork, mix

thoroughly until it resembles bread-crumbs. Dissolve
the sugar in one-third cup of water and use this to mix
the flour to a soft dough. Knead lightly, cut into pieces
the size of a small egg, and roll into balls. Flatten balls to
¼ in. thick and fry in smoking hot oil until golden brown.
N.B. Bakes may be cooked on a hot baking stone, turning
when one side has browned.

CORNMEAL BAKES 77

11 oz. (2 cups) fresh
 cornmeal
2 oz. (¼ cup) flour
1½ teasp. salt
1½ teasp. baking powder

2 oz. fat pork
½ oz. (1 tbsp.) shortening
 —lard or butter
water to bind

Chop fat pork finely, add to flour mixture, and make as
for Ordinary Bakes.

CORNMEAL ARRAPE 78

1⅓ lb. (4 cups) cornmeal
2 oz. (½ cup) flour
1 oz. (2 tbsp.) butter
1 oz. (2 tbsp.) lard

2 teasp. salt
3 teasp. baking powder
water to bind

FILLING
½ lb. beef
1 oz. fat pork
½ teasp. salt

seasonings to taste
2 tbsp. oil

Clean the meat and brown it with the fat pork and
seasonings. Cover and stew for half an hour, then
mince or chop finely. Prepare the cornmeal mixture as
for Bakes, and flatten the balls to ⅛ to ¼ in., or roll out the
mixture and cut into 2 to 3 in. circles with a cup or cutter.

Put about 1 tbsp. meat mixture on one circle, damp the edge and cover with a second circle. Squeeze the edges together and fry in smoking hot oil till golden brown. Drain and serve hot.

N.B. Flour is sometimes omitted. In this case mix cornmeal with hot water.

79　CORN FRITTERS

¼ pt. (½ glass) milk
2 cups boiled corn cut
　from the cob
½ lb. (2 cups) flour
1½ teasp. salt
⅓ teasp. pepper

2 teasp. baking powder
1 tbsp. melted butter
1-2 eggs (if only 1 egg is
　used reduce the
　quantity of flour)

Beat eggs and gradually stir in flour and milk. Add all other ingredients except baking powder and beat well. Stir in baking powder last of all. Fry spoonfuls in smoking hot oil. Drain on absorbent paper and serve at once.

80　TANNIA CAKES OR FRITTERS

2-3 small tannias or 1
　cup grated tannia
1 tbsp. flour
½ teasp. salt
1-2 blades chive

½ teasp. bicarbonate of
　soda, or 1 teasp.
　baking powder
pepper
1 egg (if liked)

Wash and peel tannias. Wash again and grate finely. Chop seasonings finely and mix all ingredients. Beat well. Drop spoonfuls in smoking hot oil. Fry till golden brown, drain, and serve at once.

PLANTAIN CAKES 81

2-3 small yellow
  plantains (not ripe
  enough to fry)

1 teasp. salt or 1 tbsp.
  sugar

½ teasp. baking powder

} to every cup crushed
plantain

Boil the plantains, peel, pound, or mash them. Mix all
ingredients. Shape into little cakes slightly larger than a
penny and fry in smoking hot oil.

PUMPKIN PANCAKES 82

½ lb. pumpkin

1 oz. (¼ cup) flour

½ oz. (1 tbsp.) sugar

¼ teasp. spice or essence

½ teasp. baking powder

} to every cup crushed
pumpkin

Wash, peel, and steam the pumpkin. Mash thoroughly
and stir in all other ingredients. Beat well and fry by
dropping spoonfuls into smoking hot oil. Dry, sprinkle
with fine sugar, and serve at once.

  N.B. Beaten egg may be added to the mixture. In this
case increase the quantity of flour by half as much
again.

FRITTER BATTER 83

2 oz. (½ cup) flour

4 tbsp. water or milk

1 tbsp. oil (if water is
  used)

1 egg white or ½ teasp.
  baking powder
pinch of salt

Sift flour, and gradually beat in oil and water. Cover and set aside for 20-30 min. Whisk egg white until it is stiff enough to stand in a point, and fold it lightly into the batter. Use for fish or fruit fritters.

Important Note
If baking powder or soda is used in place of egg, use 2 extra tbsp. water, and do not add the baking powder until after the mixture has stood.

84 BANANA FRITTERS

2-3 bananas according to the size	fritter batter as given above

Peel the bananas, cut in half lengthwise, then cut into two or three across. Coat each piece with batter and fry in smoking hot oil till golden brown. Drain, sprinkle with sugar, and serve at once.

N.B. Some people mash the bananas and make them in the same way as Pumpkin Pancakes. This is not so good, as the fritters are inclined to be heavy, indigestible, and unappetizing.

85 SALT FISH FRITTERS

| ½ lb. salt fish | pepper to taste |
2-3 blades chive	fritter batter as above

Prepare the batter. While it is standing, thoroughly scald the fish, then bone, skin, and pound or flake it. Chop the chive very finely. Complete the batter, add fish and seasonings, and drop spoonfuls of the mixture into smoking hot oil. Turn as required, and cook until golden brown—about 2-3 min.

N.B. Fresh cooked fish may be used in place of salt fish; in this case add half teasp. salt.

JAMAICA AKRAS 86

Take any quantity of Black Eye Peas and soak them
overnight. Pulp them out of the skins, add salt and
green pepper, and pound them until creamy. Drop
spoonfuls in smoking hot oil and fry till golden brown.
Drain on absorbent paper and serve hot.

ACCRA 87

½ lb. (2 cups) flour
¼ oz. yeast
½ teasp. salt
3 oz. salt fish
2 blades chive

½ small onion, garlic, and
   thyme
piece of red pepper or
  ¼ teasp. black pepper
1½ cups warm water

Scald fish twice, then remove skin and bone. Pound
fish, onion, garlic, thyme, and pepper together till fine.
Sift flour and salt into a bowl. Mix yeast to a paste with a
little of the water, then add the rest of the water and stir
it into the flour until a soft batter is formed. Add fish and
beat mixture for 2-3 min. Stand in a warm place to rise
for 2 hrs. Fry by spoonfuls in smoking hot oil. Drain and
serve hot with Floats (see recipe 88).
N.B. A smaller quantity of yeast is sometimes used. In
this case the mixture must be allowed to rise for a
longer time.

FLOATS 88

1 lb. (4 cups) flour
4 oz. (½ cup) shortening,
  e.g. lard

1½ teasp. salt.
¼ oz. yeast
warm water

Sift flour and salt together. Add shortening, and using
finger tips or a fork, mix thoroughly till it looks like fine

crumbs. Mix yeast to a paste with a little warm water, then add to the flour and shortening, adding enough warm water to make a soft dough. Knead well until smooth. Put to rise in a warm place for 2 hrs. or until mixture is twice as big. Cut into pieces the size of a small egg, and roll into balls. Put to rise again for 20 min. Flatten out to $\frac{1}{8}$ in. thickness, and fry in smoking hot oil. Drain and serve hot.

89 FRIED FISH

fillets or cutlets of large fish, or a whole small fish
seasonings to taste
bread-crumbs or raspings or farine or flour
oil for frying

beaten egg or batter made from 1 tbsp. flour and 3 tbsp. water or milk
sauce, e.g. creole butter sauce, parsley, or shrimp sauce.

Clean the fish and season it for not more than 20 min. Beat the egg or prepare the batter in a shallow plate, and put bread-crumbs or farine on a piece of paper. Remove seasonings from fish, dip each piece in egg or batter, then drain well, using two forks; toss in the bread-crumbs, place on a board, and press the bread-crumbs in place with the blade of a knife.
(N.B. If flour is used, no egg or batter is required.)
Fry at once in smoking hot oil—if left to stand after coating, the flour or bread-crumbs become saturated and do not fry so well. Turn fish if necessary, and be very careful not to put too much in oil at once, otherwise this cools the oil, and this is bound to make the fish break. Drain well on crushed absorbent paper. Arrange on a hot dish. Use the seasonings for a suitable sauce.

FRIED BEEF 90

1 lb. beef—good quality
  e.g. steak, fillet,
  tenderloin
1 tbsp. flour for coating
½ teasp. salt
⅛ teasp. pepper

6 tbsp. oil (approx.)
1 onion
1 blade chive, thyme
½ pt. (1 nip) stock or
  water

Wipe meat thoroughly, then beat it gently with a rolling-pin or bottle to bruise the fibres, and so soften the meat. Cut it into neat slices not less than 1-1½ in. thick, then cut the slices into pieces about 3 in. square or more. If the meat is cut too thin or into too small pieces, so much of the inside is exposed that the meat juice runs out, and the meat is less nourishing and less tasty.

Prepare the seasonings (cutting onion into rings), and season the meat for about 20 min., or simply rub the meat with the onion before cutting it up. Mix the flour, salt, and pepper, and coat the meat. Heat the oil till slightly smoking, put in the meat, cook quickly for the first 2 min., turning as soon as one side has browned. Then decrease heat slightly and cook meat for 10-12 min. in an uncovered pan.

When cooked the beef should be well browned and look puffy. when pressed it should dent easily but regain its shape at once. If it is not puffy and does not dent easily when pressed, this is a sign that it is overcooked.

Keep the meat hot and make a sauce. Fry the seasonings, add the rest of the flour, and brown evenly. Stir in the stock or water gradually and boil for 2-3 min.

7 Grilling

Other names for grilling are broiling or toasting, and it is done over, under, or in front of a glowing fire—for example, we can hang a piece of meat or a fish over glowing wood when we are out camping, we can put it on a grid over glowing coals, or under an electric or gas griller.

Grilling is a convenient way of cooking, because it is quick, and this short cooking does little to spoil the food value. Little oil or fat of any kind is used, so that it is more digestible than fried food. Because it is a quick way of cooking, only small tender pieces of food can be grilled, and young birds and tender meat cost more than old or tough and bony cuts.

Rules for grilling

1 Use a hot grill to brown the food quickly—quick browning cooks the protein on the surface of the meat, and this forms a thin covering which prevents meat juice from running out.
2 Heat the grid before using—this also helps food to brown quickly.
3 To prevent food from sticking, grease the grid before heating it.
4 Grease the food too. This prevents it from drying up and becoming unpalatable.

GRILLED MEAT 91

Suitable meats for grilling are mutton cutlets, beef
steak or fillet (undercut), kidneys, sausages.
Seasonings to taste, Maître d'hôtel Butter (recipe 92).

Mutton
Trim off excess fat which would simply melt. Do not
remove the meat from the bone.

Beef
Pound or beat the beef lightly to soften it. Cut into 1-1½
in. slices, and then into rounds or squares about 2-3 in.
across.

Kidneys
Wash, scald, and skin the kidneys. Cut them open along
the hollow side and cut out all tubes, etc.

Sausages
Wash and prick.

Season the meat. Usually nothing but salt, pepper, and
a little vinegar or sauce are used, but the meat may be
rubbed with onion or other seasonings, if liked. Brush
over with oil or butter, place on a hot grid, and brown
quickly. Turn as soon as one side is well browned (about
2-3 min.). Avoid pricking meat with fork or knife when
turning, otherwise meat juice will escape through
pricks. Turn by holding between two spoons or the flat
blades of two knives.
When both sides are brown, lower the heat and
complete cooking more slowly. When cooked, meat
should be brown and puffy, and if pressed the hollow
made should immediately fill up again. Put a pat of
Maître d'hôtel Butter (recipe 92) on top of both mutton
cutlets and beef. Serve at once.

92   MAÎTRE D'HÔTEL BUTTER

1 tbsp. butter	1 teasp. lime juice
2 teasp. finely chopped parsley	¼ teasp. salt
	pinch of white pepper

Wash, thoroughly dry, and finely chop the parsley. Mix all ingredients. Form into small pats and place on grilled meat just before serving. The meat must be hot enough to melt the butter. This is used instead of sauce or gravy.

93   MIXED GRILL

This is a substantial dish consisting of a variety of foods grilled and served together. Follow general rules for grilling and include such things as kidneys, sausages, ham or bacon, chops, steaks, mushrooms, and tomatoes.

94   GRILLED FISH

Use small fish or slices or cutlets from a large one. Scale, trim, and clean the fish. Butter both sides, season with pepper and salt, and , if liked, put finely chopped chive, tomato, etc., in the cavity left by cleaning.
Grill for a few minutes on both sides, turning very gently. Allow about 5-7 min. in all, depending on the size. When cooked, fish should look "set" like hard-boiled egg, and should be golden brown. Serve with creole butter sauce or a white sauce.

95   GRILLED POTATOES OR OTHER ROOT VEGETABLES

Scrub and boil the potatoes. Peel and place on a greased grid. Grill over a glowing fire, turning constantly to ensure even browning.

Baking and roasting 8

Baking is cooking in an oven or covered pot. In the old days people used both to bake and roast foods, but now very little roasting (which is cooking in front of a large open fire) is done. Many foods which are called roast are really baked, e.g. roast chicken, potatoes, etc.

Baking is a favourite way of cooking because crisp, brown baked foods both look and taste good. It is a better way of cooking than frying. because the food is more digestible.

Unfortunately baking is not a cheap way of cooking, because the food is likely to shrink and become dry, so only good pieces of tender and more expensive meat, young chickens, etc., can be baked.

Not only meat, but fish, vegetables, puddings, and cakes are all baked. An oven will, of course, give the best results, but small pieces of food can be baked in an iron pot.

General rules for baking

1 See that the inside of the oven is as clean as the inside of a saucepan.
2 Heat oven to correct temperature before putting in the food.
3 Dry food such as vegetables or fish before putting in oven.
4 If possible, save fuel by using your oven for more than one food at a time.

Oven temperatures

a	*Moderate Oven*	220°-350° F.
	Large cakes	300°-350° F.
	Egg dishes, meringues (*soupirs*)	220° F.

b	*Hot Oven*	350°-375° F.
	Biscuits	350°-450° F.
	Fish	350° F.
	Plain cakes	370° F.

c	*Quick or Very Hot Oven*	375°-500° F.
	Sponge sandwich	375° F.
	Pastry	420° F.
	Bread and Scones	450° F.
	Meat (first 15 min. only)	500° F.

If no thermometer is obtainable use the "bread test."
Put a small piece of bread in the oven; if at the end of
exactly 5 min. it is—
biscuit colour—the oven is moderate
golden brown—the oven is hot
dark brown—the oven is quick or very hot

96   ROAST BEEF OR MUTTON

1 joint good quality beef, e.g. undercut (fillet), sirloin, or
    rolled ribs, aitchbone, topside
1 joint good quality mutton, e.g. leg, shoulder, or loin
2-3 oz. (4-6 tbsp.) fat, e.g. dripping, lard or oil
salt and pepper

Wipe meat thoroughly with a damp cloth. If liked, rub it
with seasonings or pack seasonings into any
crevices—none should be left on the outside as they
will burn. Using metal skewers (meat pins) and clean
twine, tie joint into shape if necessary.

Put meat on a grid in dripping-pan with dripping or oil—if potatoes are to be cooked with meat, use the full 3 oz. oil. Put meat in a very hot oven, so that the outside will quickly brown and form a coating which will keep in the meat juice. Lower heat after the first 15 min.; the dripping should sizzle gently.

For large joints, allow 20 min. for every lb. and 20 min. over for the piece; e.g. 4 lb. joint—time allowed 4 × 20 + 20 min. = 1 hr. 40 min. For small joints of under 3 lb. allow 1¼ hrs. for thin pieces and 1½ hrs. for thick pieces. Baste meat (i.e. pour a spoonful of hot oil from the dripping-pan over the meat) every 20 min. This keeps meat moist and juicy and helps it to brown. Some people use a covered dripping-pan—in this case no basting is necessary, but remove cover 15 min. before meat is done, so that outside may be made brown and crisp. When cooked, put meat on a hot dish and keep hot while gravy is made.

PLAIN GRAVY FOR ROASTS 97

Strain dripping from pan in which meat was cooked, keeping back the brown semi-solid substances (meat juice) on the bottom of pan. Sprinkle in 1 teasp. flour and allow it to brown evenly. Add ½ pt. (1 glass) water or stock, ½ teasp. salt, and ⅛ teasp. pepper. Heat to boiling-point, and strain into a gravy tureen.

N.B. This gravy should be clear and free from fat.

ROAST POTATOES COOKED WITH MEAT 98

Peel and wash potatoes, cut in halves or quarters if large. Soak in salted water for half an hour. Dry well and put in dripping pan round meat when it is about half cooked—allow 45 min. for potatoes. Baste and turn them as they brown. When cooked they should be soft inside and crisp and brown outside. Serve in a hot vegetable dish or round the joint.

99   ROAST PORK

Choose leg, loin, or spare rib. Cook in the same way as beef, but for a longer time—allow 25 min. to every lb. and 25 min. over for the piece, e.g. 4 lb. joint, allow 4 × 25 + 25 = 2 hrs. 5 min. When it is cooked the pork should be white-looking right through. It is dangerous to eat undercooked pork. Pigs are sometimes infected with tiny worms which lodge in their muscles (the lean of the meat). It is important that we cook the pork thoroughly to make certain that the heat has completely destroyed any that may be present.

100   ROAST CHICKEN

1 young fowl
about 4 tbsp. stuffing or
   forcemeat (recipe
   325)
about 10 rashers (slices)
   bacon

gravy (this should be
   paler than the gravy
   served with beef)
½ pt. bread sauce (recipe
   253)

Pluck and singe the bird. If the bird is not very young pour hot water over it before plucking to loosen feathers and kill lice. Cut off head; make a long slit at back of neck, loosen skin and cut off neck close to body leaving skin on the bird. Cut round vent to free entrails, remove gullet, crop, windpipe, and all internal organs. Cut out oil sack above tail. Wash and dry inside and outside of bird. If liked, rub with lime juice and salt. Break legs above spur, twist and draw out sinews. Stuff the bird and fold skin over at neck. Press legs forward

close to breast and turn wings in close to the sides. See
that bird will sit flatly without wobbling, and tie legs and
wings in place. Cover breast with one or two slices of
fat bacon and place on a grid in a dripping-pan. Bake in a
hot oven for $1\frac{1}{4}$-$1\frac{1}{2}$ hrs., depending on size. Baste
frequently. To brown the breast remove bacon 15 min.
before fowl is cooked, dredge (sprinkle) with flour, and
baste. Remove string and serve on a hot dish garnished
with bacon rolls.

To make bacon rolls
Remove rind and flatten bacon rashers with the blade of
a knife. Cut into strips about 1-$1\frac{1}{2}$ in. wide and roll up.
Arrange several rolls on a skewer, put it across corner of
dripping-pan, and bake with chicken for last 10 min.

To prepare trimmings or giblets
Remove gall from liver and sac of stones from gizzard.
Scald feet and remove toes and scales. Soak feet, liver,
heart, neck, kidney ,and gizzard in warm water for 20
min., then wash well. Add about 1 pt (2 glasses) water
and $\frac{1}{2}$ teasp. salt, and simmer for 1 hr. to make stock for
gravy, soup, etc.

ROAST SUCKING PIG 101

1 prepared sucking pig,
   not more than 3
   weeks old
butter or oil to baste

stuffing containing
   olives, capers, petits
   pois, spice, etc., if
   liked

Wash the pig thoroughly in cold water and wipe dry.
Loosen and fold back skin round the feet. Cut off the
feet and turn skin back over ends. Either rub the pig with
seasonings or stuff it and sew up the opening. Draw
legs well back and tie them in place. Brush all over with

oil or melted butter, wrap it in several folds of
greaseproof paper and bake in a hot oven for 2½-3 hrs.,
according to size. Remove paper ½ hr. before pig is
ready, dredge with flour and baste well. The pig should
be crisp and brown when cooked. Place a baked potato
in the mouth and serve with plain gravy and apple (or
mango) sauce.

102 POT ROAST

Choose a small tender piece of meat
    weighing not more than 1 lb.

Wipe and season meat in the usual way, but before
roasting remove all seasonings from the outside. Put
about 4 tbsp. oil or dripping in a small thick iron pot or
saucepan—the oil should be about ½ in. deep. Heat till oil
is smoking. Put in meat, cover, and brown quickly. Turn
as required. When brown all over, reduce the heat and
cook gently for about 50 min. Keep closely covered.
Serve on a hot dish with gravy or creole sauce.
N.B. Some people add a little water when pot-roasting.
This should not be necessary if the cover fits well. If oil
is overheated a little water may be added, but care must
be taken to avoid scalds from the steam which rises
when the water is put in.

103 BAKED STUFFED FISH

1 large red fish or
    mackerel
	1 tbsp. raspings (dried
	    bread-crumbs)

2-3 tbsp. stuffing (see
    recipe 325)
	2-3 tbsp. oil, dripping, or
	    butter

Scale, trim, and clean fish in the usual way. Wash and
dry it, but omit seasoning as it is to be stuffed instead.

Prepare stuffing and fill cavity. Secure edges with a small skewer or sew them together, taking great care that the needle is not left in the fish! Put oil in a dripping-pan and heat till smoking. Put in fish, dredge top with plenty of raspings, and baste at once. Cook for 20-30 min. in a moderate oven, basting frequently. Serve on a hot dish with gravy or creole sauce.

CRAB BACKS 104

1 doz. crabs
2-3 tbsp. butter
1 chopped onion
1 tomato
2-3 blades chive

1 tbsp. Worcester sauce
   or vinegar
salt and pepper to taste
raspings (dried
   breadcrumbs) for the
   top

For good results the meat of 12 crabs should be used for not more than 8-10 finished crab backs. For the sake of economy fresh bread-crumbs or cooked fish is sometimes added to the mixture to make it go further. Obtain crabs at least one day before they are required and keep them feeding on wholesome food, e.g. bread, pepper leaves, etc., till purged. Place in a large pan and pour on enough boiling water to cover. Throw away this water, wash crabs, and boil for half an hour to loosen flesh. Remove claws, cut open and pick out meat. Remove body from shell, carefully preserving any eggs and fat, but discarding the gall which clings to the shell. Scrub shells thoroughly. Prepare seasonings, and brown them in the butter. Add flaked crab meat, Worcester sauce, salt, and pepper. Refill shells, sprinkle with raspings and a small dab of butter, and brown in a quick oven.

105 SALT FISH PIE

½ lb. salt fish
¾-1 lb. Irish potatoes
3-4 blades chive

1 large onion
½ teasp. black pepper
about ½ pt. (1 glass) milk

Soak fish well, then scald it and remove skin and bone.
Boil potatoes and parboil onion. Pound fish with
chopped chive and onion, and add pepper. Slice half the
potatoes and mash the rest with a little milk. Arrange
alternate layers of sliced potato and fish in a greased
pie-dish. Moisten with the rest of the milk. Put the
mashed potato on top, smooth with a wet knife and
decorate. Add one or two dabs of butter and brown in a
quick oven (about 20-30 min.). Garnish with slices of
tomato or hard-boiled egg.

N.B. Some people prefer to make a little white sauce to
mix with the fish.

106 SALT FISH SOUFFLÉ

½ salt fish
2 oz. (½ cup) flour
2 oz. (4 tbsp.) butter

¼ pt. (½ glass) milk
white pepper to taste
1 teasp. lime juice

Scald salt fish, and remove skin and bone. Flake or
pound finely. Melt butter, stir in flour without browning.
Add milk, and stirring continuously cook until a thick
white sauce is obtained. Add all ingredients except egg
whites, and beat well. Whisk egg whites very stiffly and
fold into mixture. Pour into a greased pie-dish or basin,
leaving enough space for mixture to rise. Bake in a quick
oven till mixture is well risen, set, and golden brown
(about 25-30 min.) or cover and steam till set (about 45-
50 min.). Serve at once.

MELONGENE AU GRATIN 107

1 melongene	onion, chive, tomato,
pepper and salt to taste	etc., if liked
1 tbsp. butter or oil	raspings (dried
	breadcrumbs)

Wash and boil melongene whole, or prick it and roast over a slow fire. Lightly fry the seasonings in the butter. When melongene is soft, cut in half lengthways, scoop out the centre and mix all ingredients. Refill the shells or pile mixture in a pie-dish. Sprinkle top with raspings, add dabs of butter, and brown in a quick oven.

PAPAW AU GRATIN 108

Choose a green papaw, wash, cut in half and remove seeds. Boil till soft and then prepare in the same way as melongene. Seasonings may be omitted if liked.

MELONGENE ROMA 109

1 medium-sized	$\frac{1}{4}$ lb. grated cheese
melongene	4 tbsp. chopped onion or
1 egg	onion and chive
1 teasp. salt	1 cup tomato sauce or 3
4 tbsp. butter or oil	large tomatoes

Wash and peel melongene, and cut crosswise in $\frac{1}{4}$-$\frac{1}{2}$ in. slices. Beat egg, add $\frac{1}{2}$ teasp. salt and coat melongene. Heat butter and lightly fry melongene till brown but not quite tender. Arrange slices in stacks of three with cheese between and on top, and place in a shallow fireproof dish. Fry onion (and tomatoes if used) and put them with sauce and balance of salt round melongene. Add $\frac{1}{2}$ cup water if no tomato sauce is used. Bake in a moderate oven till cheese browns (about 25 min.).

110   EDDO SOUFFLÉ

1 lb. eddoes
1 oz. (2 tbsp.) butter
¼ pt. (½ glass) milk

2 eggs
1 teasp. salt
¼ teasp. white pepper

Peel and wash eddoes with lime juice. Cook till soft in boiling salted water. Crush thoroughly, and mix with all ingredients except egg white. Beat well. Whisk egg white very stiffly and fold into eddo mixture. Pour into a greased pie-dish allowing room for the mixture to rise. Bake in a quick oven till well risen and golden brown—about 20-30 min. Serve at once before mixture falls.

N.B. Other root vegetables may be used in the same way. 3-4 oz. grated cheese may be added, if liked.

111   AVOCADO PEAR SOUFFLÉ

1 medium-sized pear
1 oz. (2 tbsp.) butter
1 oz. (4 tbsp.) flour
¼ pt. (½ glass) milk

½ teasp. salt
½ teasp. white pepper
2-3 eggs

Peel and grate the pear. Melt butter, stir in flour, then milk, and make a thick white sauce. Cool mixture, stir in egg yolks and beat well. Whisk egg whites stiffly, fold them into sauce mixture with grated pear. Season to taste. Pour into a greased pie-dish, allowing room for mixture to rise. Bake in a quick oven till well risen and golden brown—about 30 min. Serve at once before mixture falls.

N.B. The mixture may be steamed instead of baked; in this case, allow about ¾-1 hr., cover and steam till set.

CREAMED BREADFRUIT 112

1 ripe breadfruit
about ½ cup hot milk
1 egg

1 tbsp. butter
pepper and salt to taste

Wash and boil breadfruit. Peel and mash with salt, pepper, and butter. Add enough hot milk to make to a thick creamy consistency. Beat egg thoroughly (white may be whisked separately if liked) and stir into mixture. Pile in a greased pie-dish and brown in a quick oven or fry spoonfuls in smoking hot oil.

STUFFED BREADFRUIT 113

1 breadfruit—full but not
   ripe
½ lb. fresh beef or pork
1 thick slice raw ham or
   ¼ lb. pickled meat
1 tomato

1 small onion
2-3 blades chive
1 tbsp. butter or oil (more
   if no pork is used)
salt and black pepper to
   taste

Peel and parboil breadfruit whole in salted water. Clean meat and seasonings, lightly fry them in the butter, then mince or chop. Cool breadfruit, and from the stalk end cut out core and a little fruit. Fill hole with prepared meat mixture. Bake in a moderate oven till soft and brown—about 45 min. Butter crust and serve hot.

Alternative method
Use unpeeled raw fruit, scoop out centre, and after filling in the usual way, roast over a wood fire. Peel and butter before serving.

114   TANNIA MEGAN

3-4 tannias	1 tomato
¼ lb. salt beef (or cooked meat)	1 small onion
	1 tbsp. butter or dripping

Wash and soak salt beef. Wash and peel tannias and onion, and cook in boiling salted water. Mash tannias, and chop or mince salt beef, onion, and tomato. Mix all ingredients, beat well, and pile in a greased piedish. Score the top, add a few dabs of butter, and bake till top is brown and crisp—about 45 min.

Bread 9

Bread is something we all use daily, and because well cooked home-made bread is nicer than the bread we buy, it is something we should all know how to make.

Bread is different from other mixtures such as those used for cakes, because yeast or leaven is used instead of baking powder, and for this reason practically all the rising has to be done before baking. Baking-powder bread can, of course, be made, but it does not have such a pleasant flavour, and it dries more quickly.

Yeast

Yeast consists of tiny little plants, each made of a single beadlike cell. They are so small that we cannot see them, and so light that they are blown about in the air. When their surroundings are comfortable they grow and give off new cells by a process called "budding"—that is, they give off little shoots or buds which gradually develop into new cells, which break away from their parent. The things they need for growth are:
1 Food—generally obtained from sugar, or starch changed into sugar.
2 Moisture.
3 Warmth—bloodheat (98·4°F.) is best for them; great heat kills them, and cold stops their growth.
When mixed with food or liquid containing sugar

or starch, the yeast cells feed on the sugar and split it up into alcohol and carbon dioxide. This is what gives bread, ginger beer, or mawby its taste and its bubbly appearance.

Kinds of yeast

1   Wild yeast collected from the air by leaving sour flour paste or potato mixture uncovered. This method is unreliable because it is impossible to tell whether the flour or potato pastes contain many or few yeast cells, so that results are very varied.
2   Baker's leaven. This is simply flour paste containing yeast. It is cheap, but somewhat unreliable, because here again we cannot tell how strong or weak the yeast is.
3   Liquid yeast from a brewery—this often turns sour.
4   Pure compressed or dried yeast, which is a mass of yeast cells unmixed with anything else. It can be bought by the ounce or by the packet. It costs more, but gives the best results.

General rules for bread-making

1   Allow about 1 oz. yeast to 4 lb. flour, but always increase the proportion of yeast when using less flour, e.g. use $\frac{1}{4}$ oz. yeast to $\frac{1}{2}$ lb. flour.
2   Add 1 teasp. sugar to yeast if bread is required quickly.
3   Keep the mixture warm the whole time, so use warm water, and stand the bowl in a warm (not hot) place.
4   Knead bread very thoroughly or the yeast will not be

spread all through the mixture, and the bread will rise unevenly, and have large holes when baked.

5 Allow bread to rise to twice its size before shaping into loaves—the time will vary with the quantity. Bread that is not given time to rise is heavy.

6 Never over-rise bread. This often causes it to turn sour, because as yeast cells get weaker, they are attacked by other living cells in the air.

7 Bake bread in a hot oven so that the yeast cells are killed, and the bubbles of gas made by the yeast are fully expanded. Lower the heat after the first 15 min., and bake bread until it is crisp and brown outside and sounds hollow when rapped on the bottom.

To make pan loaves crisp, bake them without a tin for the last 10 min.

Allow 45-60 min. for a large loaf, and 35-40 min. for small loaves.

WHITE BREAD 115

1 oz. yeast	¼ lb. (½ cup) shortening, if
2 teasp. sugar	liked
¾ tbsp. salt	about 2 pt. (4 glasses)
4 lb. (16 cups) flour	warm water

Crush yeast and sugar together and add warm water. Sift flour and salt, and add about ¼ of the total amount of flour to the yeast mixture. Cover and leave in a warm place to set the sponge (i.e. until mixture is bubbly), about 1 hr.

If shortening is used, rub it into remainder of flour, using finger-tips or a fork.

Add flour to yeast mixture and knead well until a smooth elastic dough is formed. Add some more warm water if necessary, for a hard dry dough does not rise well.

Put bread in a greased or floured bowl, and grease or cut across the top to prevent a hard crust forming.
Cover and leave to rise till twice as big.
Knead lightly to avoid bursting any bubbles and, without using extra flour, mould (shape) into loaves.
Cover and prove (i.e. put to rise again for 20-30 min.).
Proving improves the shape of loaves, but may be omitted if time is short.
Bake in a hot oven, following general rules for baking.

116   WHOLEWHEAT OR BROWN BREAD

2 lb. (6½ cups) wholewheat flour	1 oz. yeast 2 teasp. sugar
2 lb. (8 cups) white flour	about 2½ pt. (5 nips)
2 teasp. salt	warm water
¼ lb. (½ cup) shortening, if liked	

Notice that there is less salt and more water than in the recipe for white bread. Wholewheat flour contains more mineral salts and is more absorbent.
Make in the same way as white bread—the mixture will probably take longer to rise. Increase the proportion of yeast for smaller quantitites.
N.B. Some people like their bread browner than this, in which case use more wholewheat and less white flour.

117   BRAN BREAD

3 lb. (12 cups) flour	1 oz. yeast
1 lb. (6 cups) bran	¼ cup molasses or
2 teasp. salt	2-3 teasp. sugar
shortening, if liked	about 2 pt. (4 nips) water

Wholewheat flour does not keep well, and partly on this account it often costs more than white flour. People who cannot afford it should use bran instead, as although it is not as good as wholewheat, bran bread is better than white bread.

Make in the same way as wholewheat bread.

CLOVER LEAF ROLLS   118

Prepare a small quantity of bread mixture in the usual way. After it has risen, shape it into a number of small balls and brush the sides with melted butter. Grease deep pie pans or small cake tins and drop three balls into each.

Prove, and bake in a hot oven for about 10 min.

ORANGE BREAD OR BUNS   119

1 oz. yeast	2 oz. ($\frac{1}{4}$ cup) sugar
1 tbsp. sugar	1 egg yolk
1 pt. (2 nips) warm water or milk	grated rind of 2 oranges
	$\frac{1}{4}$ cup of orange juice
2 lb. (8 cups) sifted flour	$\frac{1}{2}$ teasp. salt
2 oz. ($\frac{1}{4}$ cup) shortening	

Dissolve yeast and 1 tbsp. sugar in warm water. Add 1$\frac{1}{2}$ cups flour, beat well, cover, and leave to rise in warm place until twice as large. Cream butter and sugar, and beat in egg yolk. Add to yeast mixture with remaining ingredients. Mix well, knead lightly, and shape as required. Half-fill greased pans, and leave to rise again till double in size.

Follow general rules for baking—loaves will take about 45 min; buns about 20 min.

120 HOT CROSS BUNS
Makes 12 buns

1 lb. (4 cups) sifted flour
¼ lb. (½ cup) sugar
½ oz. yeast
½ pt. (1 nip) warm milk
¼ lb. (½ cup) shortening

½ lb. (1 heaped cup)
  currants
¼ teasp. salt
½ teasp. mixed ground
  spice
1 egg, if liked

Mix yeast, a little of the sugar and the milk. Add 2 cups
flour, cover, and leave until the sponge has set—about
½ hr. Clean the currants, melt and cool the shortening,
and add all ingredients to the yeast. Knead well, cover,
and leave to rise until double in size. Shape into round
buns, place 3 in. apart on a greased baking sheet. Cover
and prove for 20-30 min. Mark a cross on the top, brush
with melted sugar, and bake in a hot oven for 15-20 min.

121 RAISIN ROLL BUNS
Makes 12 buns

½ oz. yeast
2 teasp. sugar
½ pt. (1 nip) warm milk
1 lb. (4 cups) sifted flour
a pinch of salt

2 oz. (4 tbsp.) shortening
4 oz. (½ cup) sugar
about 6 oz. (¾ cup) raisins
½ teasp. ground spice

Dissolve yeast and 2 teasp. sugar in warm milk. Add 2
cups flour, cover, and leave until spongy—about ½ hr.
Add salt and the rest of the flour, mix well, and knead
thoroughly. Cover and leave in a warm place to rise until
double in size. Knead lightly and, using as little flour as
possible, roll out to a piece about 8 in. by 12 in. and not
more than ½ in. thick.

Spread with the butter and sprinkle with raisins, spice, and sugar.
Roll up tightly from the longer side and cut into slices not more than 1 in. thick. Pack these into a greased sandwich tin with the cut edge upwards. Bake in a hot oven about 20-30 min.

POTATO BREAD
122

1 lb. (5 medium) Irish potatoes	1 teasp. sugar
½ lb. (2 cups) sifted flour	1 oz. yeast

Peel, wash, boil, and mash potatoes, saving the water in which they were cooked.
Add ¾ cup of this water to potatoes. Dissolve yeast and sugar in another ½ cup water, and add to potatoes. Stir in flour, beat well, leave in a warm place till double the size.
Shape into small balls, prove, and bake in very quick oven or fry in smoking hot oil.

CASSAVA BREAD
123

4 cups finely grated cassava   2 teasp. salt

Peel and thoroughly wash cassava. Grate very finely, and pound as well, if liked. Add salt and mix well. Taking only 1 or 2 cupfuls of wet meal at a time, hold it in a strong cloth or piece of flour-bag and wring out all the juice. Crumble the meal between the palms of the hand and pass it through a fine sieve. Put a baking stone on an evenly glowing fire and sprinkle a little cassava meal on it. When the meal browns, brush the stone and put the hoop (about 5 in. in diameter) in place. Spread about ½ cup meal evenly in the hoop—thin bread is crisper and more digestible than thick bread.
As soon as steam rises shake and remove the hoop,

then flatten and press the bread into shape, using a wooden palette or large knife. As soon as the bread is firm enough turn it frequently. When thoroughly dry and stiff, stand it on edge in the sun or near a fire—this improves the flavour and prevents the bread losing its crispness.

Brown or toast, and butter before serving.

124 BAKING-POWDER BREAD

1 lb. (4 cups) sifted flour   ¼–½ pt. (½ to 1 nip) water or
4 teasp. baking powder   milk
1 teasp. salt

Sieve flour, salt, and baking powder together. Add enough milk to mix to a soft dough, but one which is firm enough to handle. Knead lightly and quickly on a floured board. Shape, put in a greased bread tin and bake in a hot oven for ¾–1 hr. Test with a skewer or knife when firm and golden brown.

N.B. All rising is done in the oven

125 CORN BREAD   (using baking powder)
Makes one 8-in. square

5½ oz. (1 cup) cornmeal   1 egg
4 oz. (1 cup) sifted flour   ¾ pt. (1½ nips) milk
2 teasp. baking powder   4 tbsp. melted
1 tbsp. sugar   shortening
½ teasp. salt

Sift together cornmeal, flour, baking powder, sugar, and salt. Beat egg and add with milk. Melt and cool shortening, add to mixture and beat well. Pour into a greased shallow pan (i.e. dripping or roasting pan). Bake in a hot oven for 25 min. Test with a skewer or knife when golden brown and firm. Cut into slices when cold.

Pastry

There are about seven or eight different kinds of pastry, but we shall deal only with the better known kinds, such as shortcrust, flaky, and puff pastry.

Rules for pastry-making

1 Use as large a quantity of shortening as you can afford.
   N.B. Remember that although plenty of shortening improves the flavour and lightness of pastry, it also makes it richer and less digestible, and at the same time much more difficult to handle, particularly in a hot climate.
2 Add baking powder (1 teasp. per cup of flour) only when using less than half the weight of shortening to flour.
3 Keep pastry very cool while mixing, to avoid melting the shortening. For this reason handle it as little as possible; use china, glass, or enamelled apparatus rather than wood (e.g. use a large bottle rather than a wooden rolling-pin and a glass or enamel topped table rather than a pastry board). Glass, china, or enamel is also easier to keep clean, and is, therefore, more labour-saving and hygienic.
4 While mixing, work in as much air as possible, both to keep pastry cool and to make it light, as air expands and raises the mixture during the baking.
5 Start cooking pastry in a hot oven (400°-420° F.).

Unless flour starts cooking at once it cannot absorb or hold the shortening. Unabsorbed shortening quickly melts out and the pastry is spoiled. When cooking large pies, etc., the heat can be reduced after the first 15 min.

Kinds of shortening

Fresh butter
Gives the best flavour, but is too expensive for regular use.

Lard
Makes good light pastry, but does not give such a good flavour.

Margarine
Gives quite a good flavour, but because it contains a lot of water it does not make pastry so light.

Dripping (from stock or a roast)
Is only suitable for savoury dishes and after all gravy has been scraped from it.
Prepared shortening such as crisco, etc., gives good results.
For ordinary household purposes a mixture of lard and margarine or lard and butter is recommended.

126 SHORT CRUST PASTRY

	Example
use half the weight of shortening to flour	8 oz. (2 cups) sifted flour
½ teasp. salt per lb. of flour	4 oz. (½ cup) shortening
	¼ teasp. salt
iced water or beaten egg and water to bind	iced water or egg and water

Sift flour and salt to aerate them. Rub shortening into flour, using tips of fingers and lifting mixture high in the bowl to work in more air. If hands are very hot use a fork. Continue till mixture looks like fine crumbs. Using a knife, stir in enough liquid to bind to a stiff dough. If too soft the pastry is sticky when rolled and hard when baked.

Knead very slightly till free from cracks and turn on to a floured surface. Roll out with short sharp strokes, rolling forwards only and turning pastry round to obtain the required shape. Keep the same side uppermost throughout, as this always has the best appearance for the outside. Roll until $\frac{1}{8}-\frac{1}{4}$ in. thick. Use as required, and follow general rules for baking.

FLAKY PASTRY 127

8 oz. (2 cups) flour	iced water
6 oz. ($\frac{3}{4}$ cup) shortening	half a beaten egg white,
$\frac{1}{2}$ teasp. salt	if liked
1 teasp. lime juice	

Sift flour and salt. Add lime juice to about 1 cup iced water. Wash shortening to remove excess salt, wrap it in a floured cloth and dry well. Divide it into four equal parts, and using one part only, rub it into flour as when making short pastry. Mix to a stiff dough and roll out to a long narrow strip about $\frac{1}{4}-\frac{1}{2}$ in. thick. Keep corners square. Take another portion of shortening and spread it in dabs over two-thirds of the strip, leaving about half an inch unspread at the edges, so that shortening is less likely to ooze out after folding. If beaten egg white is used, put dabs of it between the dabs of butter. Dredge lightly with flour. Fold in the small unspread border, then fold into three with the unspread part between the other two. Lightly press edges with the rolling-pin—this seals them so that air and shortening are less likely to work out. Put pastry aside in a refrigerator for 10 min., or wrap in greaseproof paper and put on ice. Place pastry on board so that folded sides are to right and left, roll out to a long narrow strip, being careful not to burst bubbles or force air or butter out at the ends. Continue to spread shortening, fold, seal, and roll until all shortening has been used up. Put in the refrigerator between each rolling. Use flaky pastry about $\frac{1}{4}$-$\frac{1}{2}$ in. thick. After cutting to required shape, gather scraps carefully, do not knead them, but arrange in layers, fold, and roll out. If kneaded the pastry loses its flakiness. Glaze pastry just before baking, by brushing with beaten egg or milk if a savoury dish, and with milk or sugar and water for a sweet dish. Do not glaze cut edges because it stops their rising. Follow general rules for baking. When cooked, pastry should be golden brown, and firm on top and along cut edges.

128   PUFF PASTRY

8 oz. (2 cups) sifted flour
6-8 oz. ($\frac{3}{4}$-1 cup) shortening

$\frac{1}{2}$ teasp. salt
1 teasp. lime juice
iced water

Wash and dry shortening as for flaky pastry and cut about 2 tbsp. from the piece. Sift flour and salt, and rub in the 2 tbsp. shortening. Mix to a stiff dough and roll out to a strip 6 in. long and $\frac{1}{4}$-$\frac{1}{2}$ in. thick. Put the rest of the shortening all in one large piece in the centre of the strip. Fold over both ends, turn in sides and seal all edges. Give pastry a half-turn so that folded sides are now to left and right. Roll out, fold, seal, and chill as for flaky pastry until it has been rolled and folded at least three times. Glaze and bake as for flaky pastry.

COCONUT PIE
129
Serves 3-4

6 oz. short crust pastry
(*i.e.* using 1½ cups
flour)
1-2 eggs
2-4 oz. (¼-½ cup) sugar

pinch of salt
½ pt. (1 cup) milk
½ cup freshly grated
coconut

Make pastry, roll out and line a pie-dish or deep plate.
Prick the bottom and set on ice till required.
Grate coconut. Boil milk. Lightly beat egg (it need not be
frothy), add sugar and salt and stir in hot milk and
coconut. Pour filling into pastry case, bake at once in
fairly hot oven (400° F.). Reduce heat after first 10 min.,
otherwise custard mixture will boil and curdle. Cook
until pastry is golden brown and mixture set—about 30-
40 min.

CUSTARD PIE
130

Make as for coconut pie, but omit coconut and add an
extra egg and flavouring such as vanilla or nutmeg.

PUMPKIN PIE
131
Serves 4

6 oz. short crust pastry
(*i.e.* using 1½ cups
flour)
2 cups steamed or
stewed pumpkin
1 cup sugar

1-2 eggs
½ teasp. salt
½ teasp. ginger
1 teasp. cinnamon
½ teasp. allspice

Make pastry, roll out, and line a greased plate or shallow
sandwich pan about 9 in. across. Prick the bottom and
set on ice if possible. Strain off water and mash

pumpkin. Beat eggs. Mix all ingredients and beat for
another 2 min. Pour into pastry case, place in very hot
oven. Reduce heat after the first 15 min. and bake for
another 45 min. Pastry should be golden brown and
pumpkin custard mixture set and uncurdled.

132   LIME MERINGUE PIE
Serves 6

8 oz. short crust pastry

FILLING

2 cups water	3 egg yolks
4 tbsp. cornstarch	4-5 tbsp. lime juice
2 tbsp. flour	2 teasp. grated lime peel
1 cup sugar	1 teasp. salt

MERINGUE

3 egg whites	1 teasp. baking powder,
3 tbsp. very fine sugar	if liked

Make and roll out the pastry, and line a large greased
enamelled plate or pie-dish. Prick the bottom and bake
in a hot oven till crisp and brown, about 20 min.

Filling

Put water to boil. Mix cornstarch, flour, and sugar with
an extra half cup of water, mix in egg yolks lightly
beaten and add slowly to boiling water. Cook 5 min.
(using double cooker if possible); stir constantly.
Remove from fire, add lime juice, peel, and salt. Pour
into baked crust.

Meringue

Beat egg whites until very stiff, then beat in sugar only
1 *teasp.* at a time. Add baking powder, if liked. Spread
thickly over filling. Bake in a moderate oven until light
brown and slightly crisp—about 10-15 min.

133 ORANGE PUFF PIE

6 oz. short crust pastry
½ cup sugar
3 egg yolks
juice and peel of 1
   orange

3 egg whites
½ cup fine sugar
⅛ teasp. salt
½ teasp. baking powder
3 tbsp. hot water

Make pastry, roll out, and line a greased plate or piedish.
Prick the bottom and bake till crisp and golden
brown—about 20-30 min. Mix half cup sugar, egg yolks,
and water, and cook in a double saucepan until thick and
smooth. Add orange juice and finely grated peel.
Beat egg whites till very stiff, gradually beat in fine
sugar 1 teasp. at a time, so that mixture remains stiff
throughout. Add baking powder and combine with first
mixture. Pour into baked pastry shell and bake in a
moderate oven till set and slightly brown—about 20
mins. Serve at once before the mixture falls.

GROUND-NUT MOLASSES PIE 134

6 oz. short crust pastry
½ cup molasses
¼ oz. (½ tbsp.) butter
1-2 eggs
4 oz. (½ cup) sugar
¼ oz. (1 tbsp.) flour

¼ pt. (½ glass) milk
¼ teasp. salt
¾ cup chopped parched
   nuts
½ teasp. vanilla essence,
   if liked

Make pastry, line an enamelled plate or a pie-dish and
set aside on ice. Heat molasses and butter to boiling-
point, and leave to cool. Whisk eggs, and gradually beat
in sugar and flour. Stir in the milk and salt, and then the
molasses. Add chopped nuts and essence, and pour
into pastry case. Put in a hot oven. After 10 min.
decrease the heat and cook until filling is set and pastry
is crisp and golden brown—about 20-30 min.

135 GUAVA TART

6-8 oz. short crust pastry   ½ cup sugar
   (1½-2 cups flour)   lime juice
about 1-1½ lb. guavas

Make the pastry and set aside on ice. (If no ice is
available make pastry after preparing filling.)
Wash and peel guavas; cut in half and remove seeds.
Put a pie-crust raiser or egg cup in centre of pie-dish,
then fill dish with alternate layers of fruit and sugar,
beginning and ending with fruit.
Roll pastry to an oval a little larger than dish and about-
¼ in. thick. Cut off a strip (about ½-¾ in.) from all round
the pastry, damp rim of pie-dish and cover with strip of
pastry. Moisten again and cover top of pie with pastry.
Lightly press the two layers of pastry together, raise the
pie-dish in left hand, and holding a knife with the handle
slanting under the dish, trim off spare pastry. Holding
edge in position with first finger of left hand chop edges
of pastry to give a flaky appearance. Make small
scallops with left thumb and blunt edge of a knife. Bake
in a hot oven for 20 min.; lower the heat and continue to
cook for about 15 min. Pastry should be crisp and
brown. Serve with coconut cream (see recipe 129).
N.B. Many other fruits can be used in place of guava,
e.g. apple, golden apple, pomerac, etc. As these are
rather tasteless, add 2 or 3 cloves, 1 teasp. spice or a
piece of ginger.

136 BUTTERSCOTCH PIE

4 oz. short crust pastry   1 cup milk
1 egg   pinch of salt
½ cup brown sugar   1½ tbsp. butter
2 tbsp. cornstarch   ½ teasp. vanilla essence

Make the pastry, roll out and line a greased plate or pie-dish. Prick the bottom and bake till crisp and brown—about 20-30 min.

Separate yolk and white of egg, beat yolk and sugar. Mix cornstarch with enough cold water to make a smooth paste and add to egg yolk. Boil and stir in the milk and salt. Cook mixture in a double saucepan until thick—about 7 min. Remove from fire, add butter and vanilla and cool. Whisk egg white stiffly, fold it lightly into cornstarch mixture, pour into baked pastry shell, and bake in a moderate oven till well risen and slightly brown—about 15-20 min.

CREAM HORNS 137

8 oz. flaky or puff pastry   white sugar
jam

Make the pastry and set on ice. Prepare about 8 cones—these may be of tin or stiff white paper. Brush over with oil or butter. Roll out pastry to about $\frac{1}{8}$-$\frac{1}{4}$ in. Cut strips about 1 in. wide and 20 in. long. Wind them around the prepared cones, starting from the point. Brush with milk or egg white and sprinkle with sugar. Bake in a hot oven till crisp and pale brown—about 20-30 min. Cool, put a teasp. jam in each and fill with real or mock cream (see recipe 138).

MOCK CREAM 138

3 cups icing sugar   1 teasp. essence
$\frac{1}{2}$ cup fresh butter   1 egg white

Cream the butter and gradually work in the icing sugar. Stiffly beat the egg white and fold it into the butter mixture. Flavour and freeze before using.

139   BEEF PIES

8 oz. short crust pastry (i.e. using 2 cups flour and other ingredients in proportion)

FILLING
¾ lb. beef	1 teasp. salt
2 tbsp. oil	¼ teasp. pepper
onion, chive, thyme, tomato to taste	Worcester Sauce, if liked

Mix pastry and put on ice while preparing filling. If no ice is available, prepare filling first.

Clean and cut up meat and seasonings. Brown seasonings to develop flavour, and stand on one side. Brown meat, cover and simmer for 10-15 min. (This makes it very much easier to mince.) Chop or mince it with seasonings; add sauce, if liked. Roll out pastry ⅛-¼ in. thick, cut in circles about 3 in. across and reserve the best eight for covers. Put the others in greased pie-pans, add about 2 teasp. filling, damp round edge of pastry and put on cover. Press edges of pastry together and using the sharp edge of a knife parallel with edge of pie, chop the two layers together to give a flaky look. Make a small hole to let out the steam. Bake in a hot oven till firm and golden brown—about 20-30 min., or fry in smoking hot oil (in this case use less shortening for the pastry).

140   STEAK AND KIDNEY PIE

8 oz. flaky or puff pastry	½ tbsp. flour
1 lb. beef steak	1 teasp. salt
1 sheep's kidney or ¼ lb. beef kidney	⅓ teasp. pepper
	½ cup stock or water

Wipe meat; skin, wash, and dry kidney. Cut meat into

large thin slices, and kidney into small pieces. Season meat, then roll pieces of kidney and fat in slices of beef. Coat with flour, brown, add water or stock and stew for ¾ hr. Put meat in pie-dish and cool.

Make pastry, cut a narrow strip and line damped rim of pie-dish. Damp this strip of pastry, then cover top of pie. Press layers of pastry together, trim and decorate as for guava tart, but making large instead of small scallops. Make a small hole to let out steam. Brush with egg or milk. Bake in a hot oven about 1 hr. Add stock if necessary.

VEAL AND HAM PIE 141

8 oz. flaky or puff pastry	½ teasp. grated lime peel
1 lb. fillet of veal	1 teasp. salt
4 oz. bacon or ham	½ teasp. pepper
1 hard-boiled egg	½ cup white stock
1 teasp. chopped parsley	

Make in the same way as Steak and Kidney Pie, but cut meat into cubes and arrange filling in layers. Bake ¾ hr.

RUSSIAN FISH PIE 142

8 oz. flaky or puff pastry (2 cups flour)	1 teasp. chopped parsley
	½ teasp. salt
½ lb. skinned and boned fish	⅛ teasp. white pepper
	½ teasp. lime juice
1 hard-boiled egg	

SAUCE
1 tbsp. flour
1 tbsp. butter
¼ cup milk

Make pastry and set aside to cool. (If no ice is available, prepare filling first.)

Melt the butter for the sauce and stir in flour without browning. Gradually add milk, stirring all the time, and boil till thick and smooth. Set aside to cool. Clean, bone, and skin fish. Cut into small neat pieces and add to sauce with chopped parsely, sliced egg, pepper and salt. Roll out pastry to about 8 in. square and about ¼-½ in. thick. Turn pastry so that best side is downwards, place filling in centre, damp around edge of pastry and fold in envelope shape. Decorate, brush with egg, make a hole to let out steam. Bake in a hot oven for ¾ hr.—reduce heat if necessary after first 10 min.

N.B. Salt fish or cooked fresh fish may be used in place of fresh raw fish. When using salt fish, scald it first, then skin, bone, and flake it. Omit salt from the filling.

143 SHRIMP PATTIES

Sufficient to make 8 medium-sized patties

12 oz. flaky or puff pastry (3 cups flour)	½ lb. shrimps

THICK SAUCE

3 tbsp. butter	1 egg yolk
4 tbsp. flour	½ teasp. salt
½ pt. (1 cup) milk	⅛ teasp. pepper

Make pastry and set on ice. Roll out to ½ in. thick and cut out 8 rounds about 2-2½ in. across. With a smaller cutter cut a circle out of the centre, leaving rings only. Fold small circles inside uncut pastry and roll out again. Cut 8 more circles of the larger size, damp tops and put a ring on each one. Brush top only with beaten egg or milk, and bake in a hot oven till brown on top and firm at the cut edge—about 30-35 min.

Wash and scald the shrimps. Shell them, cut open along the back and remove black thread. Melt the butter, add shrimps, cover and cook for about 7 min. without browning; shake pan to prevent sticking. Remove shrimps from pan, add flour, and gradually stir in the milk, about $\frac{1}{3}$ at a time, boiling the sauce after each addition of milk, and cooking about 7 min. in all. Cool slightly, add egg yolk, and cook again without boiling until egg thickens. Add shrimps (cut into pieces if necessary) and fill hollows in pastry cases. Garnish with parsley or cayenne. Serve hot or cold.

11 Cakes

Many people prefer home-made cakes to bought ones, and even those who don't are sometimes unable to buy what they like, so that recipes for cakes are always useful. It is not necessary to know a great many cake recipes, because if we have a few standard (or master) recipes, we can make a number of different cakes simply by changing the flavouring.

It is also possible to provide a greater variety by mixing the ingredients in different ways. There are four chief ways of making cakes:

1   *The rubbing-in method*
    Flour and shortening (butter, etc.) are mixed together till crumbly. This method is good for rather simple buns and cakes, and is also used for pastry.

2   *The batter or gingerbread method*
    Shortening is melted and cooled before being mixed with flour. This method is used for fairly plain cakes and muffins, etc.

3   *The creaming method*
    Shortening and sugar are beaten together till creamy. This is a favourite way of mixing cakes—it is excellent for rich Christmas and wedding cakes, and just as good when used for plain butter sponge or Madeira cake.

4   *Whisking or sponging method*
Eggs and sugar are beaten until stiff and frothy. This
method is used for plain sponges which are very
light and digestible, but because they contain little
or no shortening they get stale very quickly.

General rules for cake-making

1   Before starting work, collect all the bowls, spoons,
and other apparatus needed. It is inconvenient to go
back to a drawer or press with floury hands, and a
cake mixture should not stand about after beating.
Grease cake pans with a saltless fat, e.g. fresh
butter, sweet oil, lard, or margarine which has been
melted and skimmed. Flour cake pans if liked, or if to
be used for very rich cakes line them with greased
paper.
2   Use good quality ingredients—one bad egg or a little
musty flour will ruin a cake.
3   Prepare all ingredients carefully before mixing them
together:
Wash salt butter. Margaine (which is only about half
the price) can be used for small buns and
economical cakes. Sift flour several times—this not
only removes impurities, but mixes air with the
flour. Air will help to make the cake light.
Pick and clean currants, sultanas, etc. They may be
cleaned by washing and then drying in a clean towel
or in the sun, or by rubbing in a little flour which must
afterwards be sifted from the currants and thrown
away. If wet fruit is used it may make a cake heavy,
and the cake will not keep well.

4 Measure ingredients carefully. Do not use too much baking powder (or soda)—this spoils the flavour of a cake. Remember that all measures must be level.

5 Try to work plenty of air into a cake. Do this by thorough sifting and beating. Air expands when the mixture is baked, and this makes the cake rise well.

6 Bake the cake immediately the mixing is finished. If allowed to stand, the air bubbles gradually fall and the baking powder may lose some of its strength.

7 See that the oven is properly heated before putting in the cake. (See Oven Temperatures in chapter on Baking, page 62.) Small buns need a hot oven to brown them quickly.
Large cakes need a moderate oven, otherwise the outside is overcooked before the middle is done.

8 Open the oven door as little as possible, and never bang it. Constant opening cools the oven and makes the cake fall.

9 When cooked the cake should be well risen, golden brown (dark brown for a rich fruit cake), firm on top, and slightly shrunken away from the side of the pan. When it looks like this and not before, test the centre with a clean warm skewer (meat pin) or knife. If no soft uncooked mixture sticks to the skewer, the cake is done.

10 Do not leave the cake in a draught when it is first taken from the oven. Leave it in the tin for about 5 min., then turn it upside down. Loosen with a knife if necessary. Remove any paper and place right side up on a wire tray. Protect from flies.

The rubbing-in method

STANDARD RECIPE FOR SIMPLE BUNS 144

To make about 10-12

½ lb. (1 cup) sifted flour
3 oz. (6 tbsp.) shortening
3-4 oz. (about ½ cup)
   sugar

pinch of salt
2 teasp. baking powder
1 egg
2-3 tbsp. milk or water

Grease small cake tins (pie pans) and prepare
ingredients. Measure and sift flour and salt into a mixing
bowl. Add shortening, and using the finer-tips (or a fork
if the hands are hot) rub them together till they look like
fine crumbs. Lift the flour high in the bowl while doing
so—this works in more air. Stir in baking powder and
sugar. Beat egg thoroughly, and use to bind mixture to a
stiff dough. Add milk or water if needed. Knead lightly
and divide into buns. Bake in a very hot oven for 15-20
min.

ROCK BUNS 145

To standard recipe (144) add:

3¾ oz. (4½ tbsp.) currants
1 oz. (4 tbsp.) chopped
   citron or other peel

½ teasp. ground ginger or
   mixed spice

Make in usual way. Arrange in rough-looking heaps and
sift over with sugar before baking: If liked, rock buns
may be made richer by adding extra shortening and a
larger quantity of currants.

COCONUT BUNS 146

To standard recipe (144) add:
   1 cup grated coconut and 1 extra egg

147   RASPBERRY (STRAWBERRY) BUNS

Make 10 or 12 buns as in Recipe 144. After shaping, press a hole in the centre of each, fill hole with ½ teasp. raspberry (or strawberry) jam and close it up again. Brush over with milk, sprinkle with sugar, and bake in the usual way.

148   CHOCOLATE BUNS

To standard recipe (144) add:

2 tbsp. cocoa powder   2 oz. (4 tbsp.) extra sugar
½ teasp. vanilla essence

Sift cocoa powder with flour, add essence to egg, and bake in the usual way.

149   ECONOMICAL SULTANA CAKE

½ lb. (2 cups) sifted flour   ¼ lb. (⅔ cup) sultanas
4 oz. (½ cup) shortening   grated rind of 1 lime
4 oz. (½ cup) sugar   2 eggs
2 teasp. baking powder   milk or water to mix
pinch of salt

Make in the same way as standard recipe (144), adding enough milk to mix to a very stiff paste or batter. Beat well with a wooden spoon. Turn into a greased floured cake pan and bake in a hot oven for 1-1½ hrs. Decrease the heat after the first half-hour. Follow general rules for cake.

SCONES 150
To make 9 small scones

4 oz. (1 cup) sifted flour
1 teasp. baking powder,
   or ½ teasp. bicarbonate
   (baking) soda,
½ teasp. cream of tar-
   tar, or some sour milk

½-1 oz. (1 or 2 tbsp.)
   shortening
½ oz. (1 tbsp.) sugar
pinch salt
milk to mix
currants of sultanas, if
   liked

Make in the same way as simple buns (recipe 144). Mix
to a dough which is just stiff enough to roll out. Roll to
¾ in. to 1 in. thick. Cut into small rounds, brush the top
with milk and bake in a very hot oven for about 10 min.
Serve hot or cold. Split open and butter.

STANDARD RECIPE FOR ECONOMICAL 151
BISCUITS
To make 12-14 biscuits

½ lb. (2 cups) sifted flour
2 teasp. baking powder
pinch salt
1 egg

1-2 oz. (2-4 tbsp.)
   shortening
about ¼ pt. (½ glass) milk
   or milk and water

Make in the same way as simple buns, using enough
milk to mix to a dough which can be rolled out. Roll to
about ¼ in. to ½ in. thick. Cut into rounds with a cutter or
glass. Bake in a hot oven for 10-12 min.

WHOLEWHEAT BISCUITS 152

Make in the same way as standard recipe (151), but use
only 1 cup white flour and add 1 cup wholewheat flour
and 2-4 tbsp. sugar.

153   CHEESE BISCUITS

Omit shortening from standard recipe (151), and add to the flour 8 tbsp. finely grated cheese.

154   BROWN SUGAR BISCUITS

Mix and shape the biscuits in the usual way. Spread the top with butter and sprinkle thickly with brown sugar mixed with a little spice. Bake for about 15 min.

The batter or gingerbread method

155   STANDARD RECIPE FOR CAKES

12 oz. (3 cups) sifted flour

8 oz. (⅔ cup) treacle or molasses

4 oz. (½ cup) shortening (lard is often used)

2 eggs

4 oz. (½ cup) sugar (brown sugar is generally used)

1 teasp. bicarbonate (baking) soda, or 3 teasp. baking powder

½ gill (¼ glass) milk or water

Gently heat shortening, sugar, and molasses together till liquid—cool but do not allow them to harden again. Sift flour and soda together. Beat eggs well. Gradually stir treacle, eggs, and milk into flour. Beat lightly for not more than 1 min. Pour into a lined cake pan and bake in a moderate oven for 1½-2 hrs.

Follow general rules for cake-making.

GINGERBREAD 156

To standard recipe (155) add:
2 teasp. finely ground ginger
2 oz. (or about ½ cup) chopped candied peel
1 oz. (about 2 tbsp.) chopped nuts, if liked

Sift ginger with the flour. Add peel and nuts with eggs, etc. Bake as for the standard recipe (155).

PARKIN 157

Use 12 oz. (2½ cups) oatmeal instead of flour and add 2 oz. (½ cup) chopped peel to recipe 155. Divide into pieces the size of a walnut, place on a greased tray, and bake.

STANDARD RECIPE FOR MUFFINS OR SCONES 158

To make about 14-15

½ lb. (2 cups) sifted flour   pinch salt
2 teasp. baking powder   1 or 2 eggs
½ oz. (1 tbsp.) sugar   milk or water to mix
4 tbsp. melted
   shortening

Melt and cool shortening. Sift flour, salt, and baking powder together. Beat eggs well. Mix sugar, shortening, and eggs with flour and add enough milk to mix to a stiff batter. Half fill greased muffin pans and bake in a moderately hot oven for about 20 min.

159   CORNMEAL MUFFINS
To make 12

¾ cup cornmeal	4 tbsp. shortening
1¼ cups flour	pinch salt
2 teasp. baking powder	1 egg
2 tbsp. sugar	milk or water to mix

Sift cornmeal with flour, make as for recipe 158.

160   BRAN MUFFINS

⅔ cup bran	4 tbsp. brown sugar or
1⅓ cup flour	molasses
2 teasp. baking powder	4 tbsp. shortening
1 egg	pinch salt

Mix bran with flour, heat molasses and butter together, and make as for standard recipe (158).

161   CRUMB MUFFINS

Follow standard recipe (158), and use 2 cups stale bread-crumbs and only 1 cup flour.

162   COCONUT MUFFINS

Follow standard recipe (158), and add ½ cup grated coconut, use 1 egg (the shortening may be left out).

163   MOLASSES COOKIES
To make about 20

½ cup molasses	1½ teasp. bicarbonate
2 oz. (¼ cup) shortening	(baking) soda
5 oz. (1¼ cup) flour	1 tbsp. warm milk
½ tbsp. finely ground	½ teasp. salt
ginger	

Heat molasses and add shortening. Sift flour, ginger, and salt together. Gradually stir flour into molasses. Dissolve soda in warm milk and add to mixture. Drop spoonfuls of the batter on a greased baking sheet, leaving at least 1 in. between each, or thoroughly chill the mixture and when firm shape into a roll and cut slices. Bake in a moderate oven (325° F.) for about 10-15 min.

SWEET POTATO BISCUITS   164

¾ cup mashed sweet
  potato
¼ glass milk
4 tbsp. melted butter
1¼ cups sifted flour

2 teasp. baking powder
2 tbsp. sugar (omit if to
  be used with meat)
½ teasp. salt

Mix mashed potato, milk, and melted butter, and beat well. Sift and stir in the remaining ingredients. Turn on to a floured board, knead lightly and roll out to ½ in. thick. Cut into rounds, place on a greased baking sheet, and bake in a hot oven for 15-20 min. Serve as a tea biscuit, or omit sugar and use as a garnish for stews, etc.

The creaming method

STANDARD RECIPE FOR BUTTER   165
SPONGE MIXTURE

1 egg
2 oz. (4 tbsp.) shortening
3 oz. (6 tbsp.) sugar
4 oz. (1 cup) flour

1 teasp. baking powder
pinch salt
½ teasp. vanilla essence
milk or water to mix

Unless sugar is already fine, grind it with a rolling-pin. Cream (beat) sugar and butter together until white and creamy—use a wooden spoon or palette knife. Whisk eggs and gradually beat into sugar; if mixture begins to curdle add a little flour. Beat well. Sift flour and salt, and stir it lightly into the mixture, adding alternately with milk. Use enough milk or water to keep the mixture a soft "dropping consistency" (soft enough to drop from the spoon). Add baking powder and essence with the last third of flour. Turn into greased muffin tins or a small cake tin. Follow general rules for baking.

166   QUEEN CAKES

To standard Butter Sponge recipe (165) add:

2 oz. (3 tbsp.) sultanas	1 oz. (5 tbsp.) chopped
1 egg	peel

VARIATIONS

Add one of the following:

¼ cup grated coconut	2 oz. cherries
1-2 tbsp. cocoa powder	2 oz. chopped nuts
or 3-4 squares	½ teasp. ground ginger or
chocolate dissolved in	other spice
milk	1 teasp. carraway seeds

167   BANANA CAKE

4 oz. (½ cup) shortening	2 teasp. baking powder
12 oz. (1½ cups) sugar	¼ teasp. salt
2 eggs	milk to mix
1 cup mashed banana	½ cup chopped nuts, if
1 teasp. lime juice	liked
½ lb. (2 cups) flour	

Make in the same way as Butter Sponge (recipe 165). Add banana pulp before stirring in the flour. Bake in a moderate oven (350° F.) for about 30 min.

N.B. Egg white may be whisked till stiff and added separately if desired.

MADEIRA CAKE 168

8 oz. (2 cups) sifted flour	4 eggs
5 oz. ($\frac{1}{2}$-$\frac{2}{3}$ cup) shortening	2 teasp. baking powder
5 oz. ($\frac{1}{2}$-$\frac{2}{3}$) sugar	large slice of citron for
grated rind of 1 lime	top of cake

Line the cake pan. Make cake the same way as Butter Sponge (recipe 165). Bake in a moderate oven for about 1$\frac{1}{2}$ hr. Place citron on top after the first 20 min. Follow general rules.

CORNSTARCH CAKE 169

6 oz. (1$\frac{1}{8}$ cups) cornstarch	3 eggs
2 oz. ($\frac{1}{2}$ cup) flour	2 teasp. baking powder
6 oz. ($\frac{3}{4}$ cup) shortening	vanilla essence to taste
6 oz. ($\frac{3}{4}$ cup) sugar	

Make in the same way as Madeira Cake (recipe 168).

POUND CAKE OR CHRISTMAS CAKE 170

8 oz. (1$\frac{1}{3}$ cups) currants	8 oz. (2 cups) flour
8 oz. (1$\frac{1}{3}$ cups) sultanas	8 oz. (1 cup) butter
4 oz. ($\frac{2}{3}$ cup) raisins	8 oz. (1 cup) sugar
4 oz. ($\frac{1}{2}$ cup) cherries	4-6 eggs
2 oz. (about $\frac{1}{2}$ cup) shredded peel	$\frac{1}{2}$ cup molasses, if liked
	$\frac{1}{4}$ pt. ($\frac{1}{2}$ nip) brandy or rum
2 oz. (about $\frac{1}{4}$ cup) chopped nuts	$\frac{1}{8}$ teasp. soda
2 teasp. allspice	
2 teasp. cinnamon	
$\frac{3}{4}$ teasp. ground mace	} or spice to taste
$\frac{1}{2}$ grated nutmeg	

Pick and clean fruit, cut up or mince the raisins. If liked, soak the fruit in the rum or brandy. Prepare nuts and peel, and cut up cherries. Cream butter and work in sugar; beat well. Whisk eggs thoroughly and beat into sugar mixture. Sift flour and spices and stir lightly into mixture. Add fruit and soda dissolved in a little warm water. Turn into a lined cake-pan and bake in a slow oven (275° F.) for about 3 hrs.

Follow general rules.

N.B. If preferred, mixture may be covered with greased paper and steamed for 2 hrs., then baked in a slow oven (300° F.) for 1 hr.

171 SHREWSBURY BISCUITS

8 oz. (2 cups) flour	1 egg
4 oz. (½ cup) shortening	grated rind of 1 lime
4 oz. (½ cup) white sugar	

Make in the same way as Butter Sponge (recipe 165), using only enough milk to mix to a firm dough (not a dropping consistency). Roll out thinly, prick all over and cut into fancy shapes. Place on a greased tin and bake in a moderate oven till pale gold colour—about 15 min.

N.B. Any flavouring such as spice, nuts, chocolate, almond essence, etc., can be used.

172 CHEAP COFFEE AND MOLASSES BISCUITS

6 oz. (¾ cup) shortening	¼ teasp. ground
2 oz. (¼ cup) sugar	ginger
¼ cup molasses	¼ teasp. ground
¼ cup strong coffee	clove
½ teasp. bicarbonate (baking) soda	

if liked

Make by the creaming method, but stiffer than Butter Sponge (recipe 165), because the mixture must be firm enough to roll. Beat in molasses and coffee in place of eggs. Roll thinly and cut into fancy shapes. Bake in a moderate oven (375° F.) for about 10-15 min.

COCONUT COOKIES   173

2 oz ($\frac{1}{4}$ cup) shortening	6 oz. (1$\frac{1}{2}$ cups) sifted flour
4 oz. ($\frac{1}{2}$ cup) sugar	1$\frac{1}{2}$ teasp. baking powder
1 egg	$\frac{1}{8}$ teasp. salt
$\frac{1}{2}$ teasp. lime juice	2 cups grated coconut
$\frac{1}{4}$ pt. ($\frac{1}{2}$ glass) milk	

Make by the creaming method, but slightly stiffer than for ordinary Butter Sponge (recipe 165). Add coconut with the flour. Drop small spoonfuls on to a greased baking sheet, leaving 1$\frac{1}{2}$ in. between each for spreading. Do not smooth. Bake in a moderate oven for 15-20 min.

AUSTRALIAN JACK   174

4 oz. ($\frac{1}{3}$ cup) brown sugar	$\frac{1}{4}$ teasp. bicarbonate
4 oz. ($\frac{1}{2}$ cup) shortening	(baking) soda
about $\frac{1}{2}$ lb. Quaker Oats	flavouring e.g. lime juice,
1$\frac{1}{2}$ teasp. water	ground ginger, or
	essence

Cream butter and sugar. Dissolve soda in water and stir into butter. Stir in enough Quaker Oats to make a crumbly paste. Add flavouring. Knead lightly on a floured board. Press into a shallow greased tin—the mixture must not be more than $\frac{1}{2}$ in. thick. Bake in a very slow oven (250°-300° F.) until golden brown. While still warm mark in squares. The mixture will harden when cool.

The whisking or sponging method

175 PLAIN SPONGE OR ANGEL CAKE

5 egg whites
5 egg yolks
½ lb. (1 cup) very fine
   sugar
¼ lb. (1 cup) sifted flour

¼ teasp. salt
1 tbsp. juice and grated
   rind of 1 lime or ½
   orange

Whisk egg whites till stiff enough to form a peak, then
gradually beat in half the sugar, adding about 1 teasp. at
a time—the mixture should remain stiff. Beat egg yolks
and orange juice with same beater until thick and pale,
then beat in the rest of the sugar. Mix egg white and
yolk. Sift flour and salt two or three times, then lightly
fold (stir, not beat) flour into egg mixture. Pour at once
into an ungreased pan—a special tube pan with a pipe
up the centre is best. Bake in a moderate oven (325° F.)
for 1 hr. if in a deep pan, or in a slightly hotter oven for
25-30 min. if in a shallow sandwich tin or small fancy
tins.

176 CHOCOLATE SPONGE

Use ¾ cup flour and ¼ cup cocoa, and make in the same
way as Plain Sponge (recipe 175).

177 ECONOMICAL SPONGE ROLL

2 egg whites
2 egg yolks
½ lb. (1 cup) very fine
   sugar
¼ lb. (1 cup) sifted flour

pinch salt
1 teasp. baking powder
4 tbsp. cold water
flavouring, *e.g.* ½ teasp.
   essence

Sift the baking powder with the flour and salt. Make in
the same way as Plain Sponge (recipe 175), using the

water to keep the mixture to a pouring consistency.
Pour into a shallow lined sandwich pan, spread thinly,
otherwise it is difficult to roll when cooked. Bake on the
top shelf of a quick oven for 7-10 min.—slow baking
makes it crisp and difficult to roll. Tightly wring a clean
towel out of very hot water. Sprinkle with plenty of
sugar, and while the cloth is still steaming turn the
sandwich on to it. Trim off any crusty edges. Spread at
once with warm jam or jelly and roll up tightly. When
cool remove cloth and sprinkle with fine sugar.

Miscellaneous

MERINGUES OR KISSES   178

4 egg whites	½ teasp. essence ⎫
½ lb. (1 cup) very fine	chopped nuts
sugar (*e.g.* castor)	colouring ⎬ if liked
(grind the sugar if	2 teasp. baking
necessary)	powder ⎭

Whisk egg whites stiffly, and add ⅔ of sugar very
gradually, not more than 1 teasp. at a time. Continue to
whisk until mixture will pull up to peaks (points). Lightly
stir in remainder of sugar with baking powder,
colouring, and essence or nuts if they are used. Shape
with a spoon or an icing (fluting) pump on a baking sheet
lined with greased paper. Bake in a very slow oven
(about 250° F.) until firm—about 1-2 hrs. Serve alone, or
stick two meringues cases together with whipped-
cream or ice-cream. If filled in this way decorate edges
with chopped nut.

179 GROUND-NUT (PEANUT) MACAROONS

1 egg white
2 oz (¼ cup) fine sugar
5 tbsp. finely chopped
    ground-nuts

1 teasp. essence
2 teasp. cornstarch, if
    liked

Parch and shell the nuts, then finely chop or pound
them. Whisk egg white until very stiff, and gradually
beat in sugar, 1 teasp. at a time. Lightly stir in nuts and
essence, and cornstarch if a firmer macaroon is
preferred. Drop small spoonfuls on a greased baking
sheet, leaving at least 1½ in. between them. Decorate
each with half a nut. Bake in a slow oven (300° F.) till
firm—about 20 min. They will harden as they cool.

Icing for cakes

There are four ways of mixing icing (or frosting) for
cakes, and many different kinds can be made by
changing the flavouring.

To prepare a cake for icing

1   See that the top is quite flat and not rounded. If
    necessary, cut it level and then turn it upside down,
    as the uncut surface will be less crumby.
2   If overbaked grate away any dark part.
3   If no revolving icing table is obtainable, stand cake
    on an overturned plate, so that the rim of the plate
    will not be in the way when icing the sides. Stand
    this plate on a soup plate, so that you can turn it
    round more easily.

Rules for icing

1   Crush the sugar very finely, otherwise the icing may
    be lumpy.
2   Beat icing thoroughly—this makes it smooth and
    glossy.
3   See that the icing is thin enough to spread smoothly
    over the cake, but not so thin that it will run off. Test
    it on the back of a spoon—it should coat the spoon
    thickly and hardly drip at all.
4   If the cake is needed quickly, use thicker icing—it
    will not take so long to dry.

5   When necessary, smooth the icing with a large knife dipped in boiling water—smooth each place once only.

6   Dry the icing in a warm place—if put in a slightly warm oven, leave the door open—too rapid drying cracks the icing.

7   Put cherries, nuts, etc., in place before icing dries, otherwise they will not stick.

8   When piping (fluting) a pattern on the sides of a cake, wait until the coating is quite dry, otherwise the pattern slips downward. Always squeeze evenly, but stop squeezing altogether before lifting the pipe at the end of a pattern. Hold the pipe absolutely upright when doing stars, dots, etc. Draw the pipe horizontally (sideways) for leaves, writing, etc.

If possible use a stainless steel pump and pipe. Tin ones are not good because they rust easily, and aluminium ones discolour the icing because of the lime juice or acetic acid in the icing. If nothing but an aluminium pump is obtainable, see that it is brightly polished before icing is put in.

People who have no pump at all sometimes use cones made from very stiff paper. The tip should be cut in fancy shapes. On the whole these are not very satisfactory.

180   GLACÉ OR UNCOOKED ICING

½ lb. (1⅝ cups) icing (confectioners') sugar
about 2 tbsps. water
essence and colouring to taste

This is quickly made and cheap to use, but is less appetizing than the others.
Crush sugar. Add flavouring, colouring, and enough

water to mix to a thick coating consistency. Beat till smooth and glossy.

Variations
Any flavouring such as orange juice, pineapple juice, coffee essence, etc., may be used. The icing takes its name accordingly.

CHOCOLATE GLACÉ ICING 181

2 oz. (2 squares)   8 oz. (1⅝ cups) icing sugar
  chocolate, or 2 tbsp.   ½ teasp. vanilla essence
  cocoa powder   ½ teasp. butter

Boil chocolate and butter in 1 tbsp. water till creamy. Cool and continue as for uncooked Glacé Icing.

BUTTER ICING 182

3 oz. (or ⅓ cup) unsalted   1 egg yolk or
  butter   white   ⎫
4½ oz. (or 1 cup) icing   colouring   ⎬ if liked
  sugar   ⎭

This should only be made by people who have a refrigerator, as it is not appetising unless firmly frozen.

FLAVOURINGS
Use one of the following:

1 oz. (1 square) unsweetened chocolate melted over hot water
½ teasp. vanilla essence
½ teasp. almond or rose essence
2 tbsp. orange juice and grated rind of 1 orange (add extra sugar if necessary)
2 teasp. coffee essence or add ½ cup extra sugar and enough strong coffee to flavour

Beat butter until very creamy. Add egg yolk (if used) and gradually beat in finely crushed sugar. Colour and flavour to taste. If egg white is used, whisk it stiffly and beat it in after adding the sugar. This is sometimes called Japanese Icing.

183   AMERICAN OR BOILED ICING

For one half-pound cake use:

$\frac{3}{4}$ lb. ($1\frac{1}{2}$ cups) granulated sugar	2 egg whites
$\frac{1}{4}$ pt. ($\frac{1}{2}$ glass) water	1 teasp. essence

Most people agree that this is the nicest kind to eat. It is not easy to use it for piping decoration because it dries very quickly.

Heat sugar and water and let sugar dissolve without stirring or boiling. Heat to boiling-point, and boil until syrup will spin a long thread when dropped from the spoon. Meanwhile, whisk egg whites stiffly. Gradually pour syrup on to eggs, whisking all the time. If icing seems too thin, place the bowl over a pan of boiling water and stir until mixture begins to get sugary round edge of bowl. Either spread smoothly over cake or roughen icing to give a frosty appearance.

184   COCONUT COFFEE BOILED ICING

1 cup granulated sugar	2 egg whites
$\frac{1}{2}$ cup brown sugar	$\frac{1}{2}$ cup grated coconut
$\frac{1}{2}$ cup coffee	few grains salt

Make the syrup from the sugar and coffee. Continue as for American Icing (recipe 183), and add coconut and salt after mixing syrup and egg white.

MOLASSES AND NUT BOILED ICING 185

1 lb. (2 cups) granulated
  sugar
3 tbsp. molasses
¼ pt. (½ glass) water
2 egg whites

few grains salt
1 teasp. essence or lime
  juice
1 cup chopped parched
  nuts

Make the syrup from the sugar, molasses, and water.
Continue as for American Icing (recipe 183), and add
nuts and salt after mixing syrup and egg whites.

ROYAL ICING 186

About ½ lb. (1⅝ cups) icing (confectioners') sugar
1 teasp. lime juice or 1-2 drops acetic acid—to break
  down the sugar and improve the icing
1-2 egg whites
colouring ⎫
flavouring ⎬ to taste

This icing is very hard. It is the best kind for piping
(fluting).
Lightly beat egg whites—they should not be frothy. Add
about 2 tbsp. finely crushed sugar and beat again.
Gradually work in the lime juice and sugar until the icing
is stiff enough for coating. Beat well and ice the cake.
Prick any large bubbles with a darning needle, and leave
the icing to dry. Reserve the remainder of the icing for
piping, adding a little extra sugar as it must be stiff
enough to pull up to points. Prevent it from hardening
while the cake dries by covering the bowl with a damp
cloth. Beat it again before using it.

187   ALMOND ICING

½ lb. ground almonds
½ lb. icing sugar
1-2 eggs or 2-3 egg yolks

flavouring of orange or
  lime juice, essence,
  brandy, or rum

This is seldom used except on wedding or Christmas
cakes, because ground almonds are expensive. When
used it generally forms a foundation for Royal Icing.
N.B. Egg yolks are often used rather than whole eggs
where Almond Icing and Royal Icing are made together;
the egg whites can then be set aside for the latter.
Whisk egg and sugar over hot water till thick and
frothy—the basin must not touch the water or the egg
may curdle. This cooking makes the icing keep
better—it need not be done if the icing is to be eaten
within a few days. Brandy and rum also help to make
the icing keep. Add flavourings and almonds and knead
well. Sprinkle a pastry board with sugar and roll out icing
to about ½ in. thick. Shape a strip for the sides and a
round for the top. Cover the cake, doing the sides first.
Smooth out any creases with a knife, and see that there
is a sharp edge round the top. Leave to harden.
N.B. Any surplus may be used up for marzipan fruit.

Cold sweets or puddings

MANGO FOOL 188

6 common mangoes, full but not ripe
about ⅓ cup sugar

¼ pt. (½ glass) milk
1 egg } for custard
¼ pt. (½ glass) water
cream if obtainable

Wash and peel mangoes and cut up roughly. Stew mango, sugar, and water to a pulp. Sieve or beat well. Heat milk and pour into lightly beaten egg; heat again without boiling until egg thickens. Stir all the time. Cool custard and then mix with mango purée and cream. Serve in ice-cream glassses. The mixture should be of the consistency of cream.

N.B. Mashed bananas, stewed guavas, etc., can be used in place of mango.

MAMMY APPLE SNOW 189

1 large mammy apple
2 oz. (4 tbsp.) sugar
¼ pt. (½ glass) water

2 egg whites
cherries and angelica or citron to decorate

Wash and peel mammy apple, and cut up roughly. Stew mammy apple with sugar and water till soft, but not a pulp. Strain off all juice, and sieve or mash the fruit. Stiffly whisk egg whites, then lightly stir into the fruit pulp. Pile high in ice-cream cups and decorate.

190   GUAVA CREAM

about 1 pt. (2 glasses)
   guavas (pack tightly
   when measuring)
about 2 oz. (4 tbsp.)
   sugar
1 pt. ($\frac{1}{2}$ glass) water

$\frac{1}{2}$ teasp. lime juice
$\frac{1}{2}$ pt. (1 glass) milk
$\frac{1}{2}$ oz. gelatine, *i.e.* 4
   teasp. powdered or 4-
   5 sheets

N.B. Use more gelatine if no ice is obtainable.

Wash and cut guavas in half. Stew them with sugar and
water and rub through a sieve. Add lime juice. This
amount should make $\frac{3}{4}$ pt. (1$\frac{1}{2}$ glasses) purée (do not use
more than $\frac{3}{4}$ pt). Boil milk, add gelatine, and dissolve
without further boiling. Chill purée and milk separately
to prevent curdling. When cool mix the two, add more
sugar if necessary, pour into a wet mould and leave on
ice till set. Turn out and decorate with pieces of guava
cut in a decorative way.
N.B. Other fruit such as soursop, granadilla, or tinned
peaches may be used in place of guava. These require
no cooking.

191   COCONUT JELLY

1 pt. (2 glasses) milk
1-2 tbsp. sugar
1 dried coconut

$\frac{1}{2}$ oz. (4 teasp. powdered
   or 4-5 sheets) gelatine

Grate the coconut. Heat milk and pour it over coconut.
Leave to stand for about 5 min., then stir and squeeze
coconut to extract full flavour and all the fat. Strain off
coconut, pressing well. Re-heat the milk, add gelatine
and sugar, and dissolve gelatine without boiling. Pour

into a mould and leave on ice till set. Decorate with
cherries, etc.

N.B. If no ice is obtainable double the quantity of
gelatine.

ORANGE SPONGE OR JELLY WHIP   192

rind and juice of 2 oranges	½ oz. gelatine, *i.e.* 4 teasp. powdered or 4-5 sheets
2 oz. (4 tbsp.) sugar	
½ pt. (1 glass) water	2 egg whites

Wash and peel oranges very thinly. Add gelatine, sugar,
and orange peel to water, and heat without boiling till
gelatine dissolves. Strain, add orange juice, and cool.
Add egg whites to mixture, place over a bowl of ice and
whisk till stiff—about 15 min. Pile at once in a dish. Keep
in a refrigerator till required. Decorate with cherries or
sections of orange. If preferred pour into a mould after
whisking. Set on ice, and turn out when firm.

N.B. Packet jelly, which is already flavoured, may be
used if liked. In this case use only half the packet, place
in a measure and make up to ½ pt. with boiling water.
Use no gelatine or orange. Add egg white, and proceed
as above when jelly is cool.

FRUIT SALAD   193

1 banana
1 orange
1 grapefruit   } or other fruit to taste
1 apple
piece of papaw
a few cherries

6 oz. (about ¾ cup) sugar   } syrup
¾ pt. (1½ glasses) water

Boil sugar and water together till a thin syrup is formed.
Set aside to cool. Wash and peel fruit, discard seeds,
and cut all into neat pieces. Mix fruit in a glass dish. Pour
on the syrup, of which there should be enough to float
fruit. Chill before serving.

194 BLANCMANGE OR CORNSTARCH JELLY

2 oz. (6 tbsp.) cornstarch
about 1 tbsp. sugar
1 pt. jases) milk or milk and water

FLAVOURING
One of the following may be used:

essence
1 stick chocolate or 1
    tbsp. cocoa powder

lime peel
bay leaf   heated with
spice   the milk

Mix cornstarch and sugar (and cocoa powder if used) to
a paste with a little milk. Boil the remainder of the milk
and stir cornstarch. Pour back into pan, boil again for at
least 7 min., stirring all the time. (If cooked for a shorter
time, cornstarch is not digestible). When making larger
quantitities use a double cooker, and cook twice as
long. Pour into a wet mould and leave till set. Turn out
into a glass dish.

195 TRIFLE

5-6 sponge cakes or
    enough stale plain
    cake to fill a medium-
    sized glass dish
jam or tinned or stewed
    fruit

about 2 tbsp. sherry,
    rum, or brandy
½ cup milk or fruit juice
½ pt. custard
cherries and angelica or
    citron to decorate

Slice sponge cakes, spread with jam, and pack into a

glass dish. If fruit is used place between layers of sponge cake. Moisten with sherry or rum mixed with milk or fruit juice. Prepare either custard from powder (follow directions on tin) or egg custard.

To make egg custard lightly beat 2 eggs with 1 tbsp. sugar. Heat ½ pt. (1 glass) milk and stir into eggs. Return to pan and cook until eggs thicken, but do not let mixture boil or it will curdle. Stir all the time. Cool custard and pour over sponge cakes. Decorate before serving. Use ice-cream glasses instead of one larger dish, if liked.

See also recipes:
178 Meringues
Ice-creams, pages 125–132

Hot sweets or puddings

BREADFRUIT PIE OR SOUFFLÉ 196

2 cups breadfruit (cooked and strained)
½ cup sugar
½ teasp. salt
½ teasp. nutmeg
½ teasp. ground ginger
2–3 eggs
1 cup milk
½ cup cream, if obtainable

Steam or boil breadfruit, strain, then sieve or mash. Mix all ingredients except egg white. Whisk egg white stiffly and fold lightly into mixture. Pour into a greased dish which may be lined with uncooked pastry, if liked. Bake in a moderate oven until well risen and golden brown—about 45 min. If pastry is used, have oven very hot for first 15 min.

197   SWEET POTATO PUDDING

3 cups freshly boiled
  sweet potatoes
¼ teasp. salt
2 teasp. honey or 1 tbsp.
  sugar

3 tbsp. butter
juice of 1 large orange
2 eggs
sherry or brandy, if liked
cherries to decorate

If possible crush potatoes through potato masher
(ricer), otherwise use a fork. Measure after crushing.
Add all ingredients except egg whites and beat
thoroughly. Whisk egg whites very stiffly and fold into
mixture. Heap small moulds of the mixture on a greased
baking sheet or turn into a greased pie-dish. Bake in a
quick oven till golden brown. Decorate with cherries.

198   FRUIT CHARLOTTE

5-6 apples or other fruit,
  e.g. pomerac or
  banana
3 tbsp. golden syrup
2 tbsp. water

grated rind and juice of 1
  lime, or spice to taste
½ cup bread-crumbs
2 oz. (4 tbsp.) brown
  sugar

Wash, peel, and slice fruit very thinly. Remove seeds,
etc. Grease a pie-dish, and fill dish with alternate layers
of fruit and bread-crumbs, packing tightly. Begin and
end with bread-crumbs. Heat all other ingredients and
pour over fruit. Bake 1¼ hrs. in moderate oven.
N.B. If no golden syrup is obtainable, use more sugar.

199   TROPICAL DELIGHT PUDDING

4-5 bananas
juice of 1 orange

4 tbsp. brown sugar
½ cup grated coconut

Peel bananas, cut in half lengthways, and arrange in a
greased pie-dish. Mix sugar and orange juice, and pour

over bananas. Sprinkle thickly with coconut. Bake in a
quick oven till bananas are soft and coconut is brown.
Serve at once.
N.B. Jam put between layers of banana may be used
instead of sugar.

QUEEN OF PUDDINGS   200

¼ pt. (½ glass) bread- crumbs	1 tbsp. sugar
½ pt. (1 glass) milk	1 oz. (2 tbsp.) butter
grated rind of 1 lime	2 egg yolks
	2 tbsp. jam

MERINGUE
2 egg whites   4 tbsp. fine sugar

Heat milk, add crumbs, butter, lime rind, and sugar.
Cover and leave to stand about 20 min. for crumbs to
soften. Stir in egg yolks, pour into a greased dish, and
bake in a moderate oven till set—about ¾ to 1 hr.
Remove from oven and spread top with jam. Whisk egg
whites very stiffly, then beat in very fine sugar, 1 teasp.
at a time. Pile meringue on top of jam, sprinkle with
sugar and bake in cool oven till crisp.

BREAD AND BUTTER PUDDING   201

3-4 slices bread and butter	nutmeg or vanilla essence
1-2 tbsp. currants and sultanas	1 egg
1 tbsp. sugar	½ pt. (1 glass) milk

Pick and wash currants, prepare bread and butter.
Arrange bread, currants, and sugar in layers in greased
pie-dish, beginning and ending with bread. Lightly beat

egg, add milk and flavouring, and pour over bread.
Leave to soak 30 min. Bake in a moderate oven till set
and brown on top—about 40 min.

202 RICE PUDDING

2 oz. (4 tbsp.) rice	about 2 tbsp. sugar
2 pt. (4 glasses) milk	nutmeg

Pick and wash rice. Mix all ingredients in a greased pie-
dish. Bake in a moderate oven till rice is soft and top is
brown—about 1½-2 hrs. Stir during the first half-hour.
N.B. If pudding is required in a hurry boil rice in usual
way, then mix with milk and sugar and brown in a quick
oven. This method is not as good—the rice is not so
nourishing or creamy, because it is swelled with water
instead of milk.

203 CASSAVA PUDDING OR PONE

2 medium-sized sweet cassavas	6 oz. (¾ cup) sugar
1 small dried coconut	½ teasp. ground spice and clove
2 tbsp. butter	½ teasp. essence
1 teasp. baking powder	

Peel, wash, grate, and mix cassava and coconut. Work
in butter with a fork. Add sugar, baking powder, and
flavouring, and enough water to bind stiffly. Put in a
greased dripping-pan—the mixture should be about 1½
in. to 2 in. thick. Bake in a moderate oven till crisp and
brown, about 1¼ hr. Cut into 2 in. to 2½ in. squares before
serving.
N.B. This mixture is always rather heavy. It is therefore
filling but not very digestible. Some people cook and
mash the cassava before using it.

CORNMEAL PUDDING 204

cup cornmeal or freshly grated corn	1½ pt. (3 glasses) milk or milk and water
oz. (4 tbsp.) butter	¼ cup (4 tbsp.) molasses
oz. (4 tbsp.) sugar	½ cup raisins
inch of salt	grated nutmeg and spice

Clean raisins. Heat milk and stir in the cornmeal. Mix all ingredients and beat well. Pour into a greased pie-dish, and bake about 2¼ hrs. Serve hot or cold.

FARINE PUDDING 205

cup farine	½ pt. (1 glass) milk
inch salt	spice or essence to flavour
cup sugar	

Mix all ingredients in a greased pie-dish. Soak for ½ hr. Bake in a moderate oven till farine has softened and thickened milk, and till top of pudding is golden brown—about 2 hrs. Serve hot or cold.

See also the following recipes:

14 Ice-creams

Both water ices or thickened ice-creams are most refreshing in a hot climate like ours. We have so many juicy fruits that there are many kinds of ice-creams that we can make.

General rules

Allow about 1 qt. for 8-10 servings.
Flavojr mixtures strongly, as freezing weakens the flavour.

Using a freezer

1 See that the freezer is clean and free from rust. After using it wash and dry metal parts thoroughly, but leave a little water in the wooden pail, otherwise the seams may open and make it leak.
2 Do not fill container more than two-thirds full. The quantity of ice-cream always increases as it is beaten.
3 Let the ice-cream mixture cool before you put it in the freezer or you will waste the ice.
4 Use coarse freezing salt (1 part salt to 6 parts ice) in preference to kitchen salt which does not last so long.
5 Pack freezer with alternate layers of ice and salt, beginning and ending with ice.

Turn until mixture is stiff, then open container very carefully so that no salt gets into it. Remove beater, cover and pack tightly with newspaper and an ice-blanket or bag. Keep in a cool place till required.

Using a refrigerator

Beat or whisk well before freezing—add stiffly beaten egg white if possible.
Pour mixture into trays used for ice cubes and freeze in freezing cabinet (froster).
When mixture is solid for 1 in. all round edge of tray, remove and beat it again, being as quick as possible.
Put it back in the froster and finish the freezing.
N.B. If you do not beat it, the ice-cream will freeze unevenly and be gritty.

Thickening ice-creams

or three quarts liquid use one of the following:
¼ lb. (¾ cup) cornstarch or custard powder. Mix cornstarch to a paste with a little cold liquid. Boil remainder of liquid, then stir the two together. Boil in a double cooker for 15 min., otherwise cornstarch will not be digestible.
   N.B. Cornstarch may be cooked with only part of the liquid (e.g. water), and then combined with condensed milk, fruit juice, etc., after boiling.
1½ oz. (6 tbsp.) flour. Prepare in the same way as cornstarch.
½ oz. (4 sheets or 4 teasp. powdered) gelatine. Dissolve gelatine in a little hot water and stir into mixture.
4 eggs. Beat eggs lightly. Boil 2 pints (4 glasses) of

milk and pour into eggs. Return to pan and stir over
stove till eggs thicken. Avoid boiling mixture or eggs
will curdle.

N.B. If cream or undiluted tinned milk is used, very little
or no thickening is required.

206   COCONUT ICE-CREAM

For a 3-quart freezer

2 medium-sized coconuts
1 tin evaporated milk ⎫ or ⎧ 2 pt. (4 glasses) boiled
1 tin condensed milk ⎭   ⎩   cow's milk
1 lb. (2 cups) sugar if fresh milk is used
thickening in proportions given above

Peel and grate coconut, and to it add 1½ pints (3 glasses)
water. Mix well to extract milk, then strain through a
fine cloth or sieve. Heat the milk, thickening, and sugar
together, and add coconut mixture. Keep pouring this
backwards and forwards from one vessel to another
until cool; this emulsifies the globules of fat from the
coconut and makes the mixture more appetising and
digestible. Strain into freezer. Follow general rules for
freezing.

207   GUAVA ICE-CREAM

For a 3-quart freezer

12 full guavas
1 tin evaporated milk ⎫ or ⎧ 2 pt. (4 glasses) boiled
1 tin condensed milk ⎭   ⎩   cow's milk
about 1 lb (2 cups) sugar if cow's milk is used
thickening in proportions given above

Wash guavas and put to boil in an unchipped enamelled
or brightly polished aluminium pan with 2 pints (4
glasses) water. (When boiled this should have reduced

o about 1½ pints.) After boiling about 1 hr. strain,
sweeten, and thicken guava juice. When quite cold
(otherwise mixture will curdle) add milk. Follow general
rules for freezing. When serving, decorate with pieces
of red guava from which seeds have been removed.

SOURSOP ICE-CREAM 208

For 3-quart freezer

1 medium-sized soursop—full and ripe
1 pinch of salt
1 tin evaporated milk ⎫ or ⎧ 2 pt. (4 glasses) boiled
1 tin condensed milk ⎭   ⎩ milk
about 1 lb. sugar if cow's milk is used
thickening in proportions given above

Peel soursop, mash in a bowl, and add 1 pint (2 glasses)
water and a piece of lime peel. Mix thoroughly to extract
flavour, then strain off the juice. Add another ½ pt. (1
glass) water to the pulp, squeeze and strain again to be
sure that all the flavour is extracted. Add milk, sugar,
thickening, and salt to juice. Strain into freezer and
follow general rules.

GRANADILLA (OR BARBADEEN) 209
ICE-CREAM

Make in the same was as Soursop Ice-cream

ORANGE ICE-CREAM 210

For a 3-quart freezer

Juice of 6 oranges—about 1 pt. (2 glasses)
1 tin evaporated milk ⎫ or 2 pt. boiled milk
1 tin condensed milk ⎭
about 1 lb. sugar
thickening in proportions given on page 126

Heat milk, sugar, and thickening together. Prepare
orange juice. Chill milk and juice separately. When both
are quite cold, mix and freeze in the usual way. If mixed
unchilled, the acidity of the orange will curdle the milk.

211   ORANGE WATER ICE
Serves 4-6
Small quantity for a refrigerator

3 oranges	¼ lb. (½ cup) sugar
juice of 1 lime	1 pt. (2 glasses) water

Heat sugar and water to boiling-point and skim well.
Wash and thinly peel the oranges and add peel to sugar
and water. Simmer 5 min. Strain and add orange and
lime juice. Follow general rules for freezing.

212   PINEAPPLE MILK SHERBET
Serves 6-8
A small quantity for a refrigerator

1¼ cups chopped pineapple	½ lb. (1 cup) sugar
1 pt. (2 glasses) boiled milk	juice of 1 lime
	juice of ½ orange

Prepare pineapple, reserving a few pieces for
decoration. Mix fruit juice and pineapple. Dissolve sugar
in the milk. Chill pineapple and milk separately to
prevent curdling. When cold, beat the two together.
Follow general rules for freezing.
N.B. If a thickened mixture is preferred, dissolve 1 teasp.
gelatine in the milk or make a custard using 1 egg.

BANANA ICE-CREAM 213

Serves 6-8

A small quantity for a refrigerator

2 crushed bananas	2 eggs
juice of 1 lime	1 tin evaporated milk
1½ teasp. vanilla essence	½ pt. (1 glass) cow's milk
4 oz. (½ cup) sugar	pinch of salt

Heat cow's milk and sugar together and pour on to
beaten egg yolks. Stir over the heat until eggs thicken,
but avoid boiling. Whisk egg whites stiffly. Mix all
ingredients together, stirring in egg whites last of all.
Follow general rules for freezing. Decorate with
chopped nuts before serving.

MANGO ICE-CREAM 214

Serves 8-10

Small quantity for a refrigerator

½ pt. (1 glass) fresh mango pulp put through a sieve	1 egg or 1 teasp. powdered gelatine to thicken
1 pt. (2 glasses) cow's milk	¼ lb. (½ cup) sugar
1 tin evaporated milk	few drops lime juice
	colouring, if liked

Prepare mango pulp and chill. Prepare custard from egg
and milk, or thicken with gelatine. Mix all ingredients
and follow general rules for freezing.

VANILLA ICE-CREAM 215

1 pt. (2 glasses) cow's milk	2 eggs
1 tin evaporated milk or condensed milk or 1 cup cream	4 oz. (½ cup) sugar (less if condensed milk is used)
	vanilla essence

Heat milk and sugar and pour on to well-beaten egg yolks. Stir over heat till custard thickens. Whisk egg whites stiffly. Mix all ingredients, adding the egg whites last. Add nuts, etc., or serve with sweet hot sauce, if liked.

216 PEANUT ICE-CREAM

Prepare a custard foundation. Sweeten to taste and add chopped parched nuts. Follow general rules for freezing.

N.B. Cherries or stewed and chopped prunes may be used in the same way.

When small quantities of ice-cream are to be used as a sweet (dessert) they are often served with fresh or tinned fruit or with a hot sweet sauce.

217 PÊCHE MELBA

Put half a peach in each ice-cream glass. Add a large spoonful of vanilla ice-cream. Decorate with very thick coloured fruit syrup and chopped nuts.

218 PEPPERMINT SAUCE

½ lb. (1 cup) sugar   peppermint flavouring
¼ pt. (½ glass) water   green colouring

Boil sugar and water in an uncovered pan till a thick syrup is formed. Add colouring and flavouring. Pour while still hot over stiffly frozen ice-cream. Serve immediately.

AVOCADO PEAR ICE-CREAM 219

Sufficient to make 1 quart

2 eggs
½ lb. (1 cup) sugar
1 pt. (2 glasses) milk
2 medium avocado
  pears

½ teasp. vanilla or almond
  essence, or other
  flavouring to taste

Lightly beat eggs, add milk and half sugar, and cook in a
double boiler until custard thickens. Add vanilla essence
and cool mixture. Peel, stone, and mash pears (there
should be about 1½ cups pulp) and add remaining sugar
and almond essence. Thoroughly mix custard and pear
purée. Follow general rules for freezing in a refrigerator.

CHOCOLATE SAUCE FOR ICE-CREAMS 220

4 oz. plain chocolate or ½
  cup flaked breakfast
  chocolate

about ¼ glass milk
½ tbsp. thick sugar syrup,
  if liked

Dissolve chocolate in the milk. Add syrup if used. Serve
very hot.
N.B. The sauce should be thick.

15 *Sweets, candies, and sugar cakes*

221 **PINEAPPLE CHEESE OR FUDGE**

1 pineapple   1 lb. (2 cups) granulated
                                              sugar

Peel and grate pineapple, remove all eyes. Add sugar
and heat slowly till sugar dissolves. Boil fast till syrup
spins a strong thread. Beat for about 5 min., pour into a
greased pie-dish or tin. Cut into squares when cool.

222 **GUAVA CHEESE**

Wash, peel, and rub ripe guavas through a sieve. Add 1
cup sugar to every cup pulp. Boil until mixture begins to
shrink from the sides of the pan, stirring continuously.
Test a little in cold water; if it forms a ball pour the
mixture into a greased dish. When firm cut in squares
and toss in fine sugar.
N.B. The pulp left after making guava jelly can be used
instead of fresh guavas, but neither taste nor colour is
as good.

223 **MOLASSES CAKES OR TULOONS**

1 cup molasses   flavouring, e.g. piece of
2 oz. (¼ cup) sugar   orange peel, spice,
1¼ cup grated coconut   ginger, or bay leaf

Boil molasses, sugar, and flavouring until syrup spins a

long thread when dropped from a spoon. Remove
flavouring and add coconut. Beat well, and as it begins
to thicken drop spoonfuls on a wet tin or banana leaf.
Leave to cool.

N.B. One cup parched ground-nuts or cashew nuts
may be added. Remove skins from cashew nuts by
scalding them. Tuloons made with nuts tend to spread;
if necessary re-shape them before they are quite cold.

PULLED GROUND-NUT MOLASSES 224

½ lb. (1 cup) brown sugar	¼ glass water
1 oz. (2 tbsp.) butter	pinch cream of tartar or
2 tbsp. chopped parched	squeeze lime juice
nuts	1 tbsp. molasses

Boil all ingredients except nuts. Occasionally stir very
gently. Test by dropping a small spoonful into cold
water; when cooked it should form a hard ball. Pour the
syrup into a greased tin and sprinkle the nuts over it.
When the edges are a little firm, fold them in over the
nuts. As soon as the mixture is cool enough to handle,
oil the fingers, and lightly and evenly pull the candy for
8-10 min. Cut into pieces and leave to harden.

ORANGE OR LIME TOFFEE 225

1 lb. (2 cups) granulated	2 oz. (4 tbsp.) butter or
sugar	margarine
juice of 1 lime or ½ orange	

Melt butter, stir in sugar and juice. Boil for about 10
min., stirring gently. Test by dropping a little toffee in
cold water; it should set and break with a snap. Pour
into a greased tin. When half set mark in squares.

226 PLAIN VANILLA CARAMELS

1 lb. (2 cups) granulated
    sugar
3 tbsp. condensed milk
½ teasp. cream of tartar

1 oz. (2 tbsp.) butter or
    margarine
2 in. piece vanilla bean
¼ pt. (½ glass) water

Boil sugar, vanilla, cream of tartar, and water till it forms
a hard ball when tested in cold water. Add milk, and
butter in small quantities, letting each piece dissolve
before adding the next. Boil again till it forms a hard ball
when tested. Pour into a greased tin and mark in
squares when half set.

227 COCONUT ICE OR SUGAR CAKE

1 lb (2 cups) granulated
    sugar
¼ pt. (½ glass) water

1 cup grated coconut
essence } to taste
colouring }

Boil sugar and water together. Test with a piece of
twisted wire bent into a small ring; dip this into the
syrup and blow through the ring; if small bubbles form,
the syrup is ready. If no wire is obtainable drop a little
syrup into cold water—it should form a very soft ball.
Remove syrup from fire and beat until it begins to look
"grainy." Stir in coconut, and as soon as the mixture
begins to thicken pour half into a greased tin about 10 in
by 6 in. Colour the remainder and quickly pour over the
first half. When cool, but not hard, cut into blocks.

CHOCOLATE FUDGE 228

1 lb. (2 cups) sugar
    (brown or white)
¼ pt. (½ glass) fresh milk or
    3 tbsp. condesned
    milk, in about ¼ glass
    water

1 tbsp. cocoa powder or
    2 tbsp. grated
    chocolate
1 teasp. vanilla essence
1 oz. (2 tbsp.) butter or
    margarine

Melt sugar in the fresh milk or with just enough water to
cover it. Add cocoa mixed to a paste with the
condensed milk or with very little water. Boil for about
10 min. or until the mixture will set into a soft ball when
tested in cold water. Stir occasionally. When cooked,
add butter and essence, beat lightly, then pour into a
greased tin. When cool, but not hard, cut into blocks.
N.B. Chopped nuts, grated coconut or cherries, etc.,
may be used in place of chocolate.

MARSHMALLOWS 229

1 lb. (2 cups) granulated
    sugar
1 oz. (8-10 sheets)
    gelatine
¾ pt. (1½ glasses) water

1 teasp. cream of tartar
½ teasp. essence
1 egg white
colouring, if liked
icing sugar to coat

Melt sugar in 1 glass water. Mix cream of tartar to a
paste with about 1 tbsp. water, add to sugar and boil for
about 20 min. or until the syrup forms a hard ball when
tested in cold water. Break gelatine into small pieces
and soak for 15 min. in the rest of the water (½ glass).
Add to syrup and stir until dissolved. Set aside to cool
slightly. Whisk egg white very stiffly and gradually beat

in the syrup. Continue to beat until mixture is stiff. Add colouring. Pour into a tin lined with paper and thickly sprinkled with icing sugar. Sprinkle top with icing sugar, cover with paper, and press with a weight until set. Cut in squares and roll each piece in icing sugar.

N.B. Chopped nuts, cherries, etc., may be added with the egg.

TEA   **230**

Tea is made from the dried leaves of the tea bush. Buy a good quality, because cheap teas are often mixed with pieces of stalk or inferior leaves. Cheap tea will be weak and has a poor taste, so that extra tea has to be used. "Brick" or block tea is compressed tea made from inferior leaves, stalk, and tea dust. Although cheap it is hardly worth buying, because it has little taste and little strength.

To make tea for a few persons allow:

1 heaped teasp. good tea per person
1 heaped teasp. good tea for the pot
about 1 cup boiling water per person

For large numbers use less tea per person—for example, $\frac{1}{4}$ lb. tea will do for about 50 people.
The water must be boiling in order to draw out the full flavour of the tea, and it must be freshly boiled, otherwise it gives the tea a "flat" taste. Warm the teapot with a little boiling water. Pour off this water and put in tea. Carry teapot over to the fire and pour boiling water on to the leaves. Allow to stand about 4 min. and then use. (Some people strain the tea into a fresh warm pot at this stage.) Serve tea hot with cold, boiled, or pasteurized milk, cream, or tinned milk. Serve sugar separately for those who like it.

231   ICED TEA

Make the tea in the usual way and strain after it has
stood for 4 min. Chill thoroughly and just before serving
add a lump of ice and a slice of lime.

232   COFFEE

Coffee made from the berries of the coffee bush must
be freshly roasted and ground and kept in a tin with a
tightly fitting cover or it will lose its flavour. The
stimulating part of coffee, called caffeine, upsets some
people, and for this reason a few firms now sell coffee
from which caffeine has been removed.

Coffee can be made in several ways—using a jug, a
saucepan, an ordinary percolator or a "drip" percolator.
Whichever method is used, remember that fast or long
boiling makes coffee bitter.

To make coffee for a few persons allow:
1 tbsp. coffee per person
pinch of salt
about ⅓ of a pint of freshly boiled water
about ⅓ of a pint of boiling milk

Use a smaller proportion of coffee for large numbers.
Where no percolator is available, measure coffee and
salt into a hot fireproof jug or pan. Pour on boiling water,
cover and infuse (draw) in a warm place for 10-15 min.
Heat just to boiling-point, throw in a dash of cold water
to settle the grounds, and strain into a hot coffee pot
through a very fine strainer or a piece of muslin or
flannel. Serve hot milk and sugar separately.

ICED COFFEE 233

Condensed milk or a mixture of milk and egg is
sometimes used instead of boiled milk. Make coffee in
the usual way, sweeten, add milk and chill thoroughly.
Serve in small galsses.

COCOA 234

Cocoa as well as being stimulating is a true food,
because it contains some starch and fat. It is, therefore,
a good drink for children or people doing hard work.

The amount of cocoa required per cup varies with the
kind used.

For one cup use:

1 stick cocoa or
chocolate sold in the
market, or 1 heaped
teasp. cocoa powder

$\frac{1}{2}$-$\frac{3}{4}$ cup boiling water
boiled or condensed milk
sugar if necessary

Mix cocoa and sugar with boiling water, and boil it for 2-
3 min. Most people forget to do this, and the starch in
cocoa is then raw and causes indigestion. Add milk.
Remember that the more milk and the less water you
use, the better the cocoa will be.

Fruit drinks, etc.

LIME SQUASH 235

4-6 limes according to
size

3-4 tbsp. sugar
1 qt. (4 glasses) water

Wash limes and squeeze juice from them. Dissolve
sugar in about 2-3 tbsp. boiling water. Mix all
ingredients and add ice just before serving. If limes are

scarce use some of the peel to increase the flavour.
Wash, peel very thinly, so that only green and no white
skin is used; use 3-4 strips only and add to sugar. Pour
on boiling water, cover, and infuse 10 min., then strain.

236   ORANGE OR GRAPEFRUIT SQUASH

These can be made in the same way as lime squash, but
less sugar will be needed. Orange squash is improved
by the addition of a little lime juice. Sour (Seville)
oranges, which are so often left to rot on the tree, make
a very refreshing drink—these need more sugar.

237   PINEAPPLE DRINK

peelings from 1 pineapple	2 cloves
about 1 qt (4 glasses) boiling water	small piece dried orange peel, if liked
	sugar to taste

Put peelings, cloves, and orange peel in a jug and pour
on boiling water. Cover and leave for 1 day. Strain and
sweeten. Use at once or bottle and keep 1-2 days.
N.B. When pineapples are plentiful the pulp may be
chopped and used with the peel.

238   COCONUT DRINK

Thoroughly chill the water from a green coconut. Add a
little gin, if liked.

239   GUAVA DRINK

about 1 large handful guavas	sugar to taste
1 qt. (4 glasses) boiling water	small piece dried orange peel

Wash and cut up guavas. Prepare as for pineapple drink.
Do not leave for more than 1-2 days in bottles,
otherwise they will burst.

SOURSOP PUNCH 240

1 medium-sized soursop
about 1½ pt. (3 glasses)
   cold water
1 strip lime peel

enough condensed milk
   or sugar to sweeten
pinch of salt

Wash and peel soursop, mash in a bowl with lime peel.
Gradually stir in 1 pt. water. Mix well and strain. Add
another half pint water, and squeeze and strain again to
be sure that all flavour is drawn out. Add salt and
condensed milk or sugar. Chill before serving.

PONCHE DE CRÈME 241

half tin condensed milk
¼ pt. (½ nip) rum
3 eggs

sugar and essence to
   taste
few drops lime juice

Beat all ingredients lightly. Add crushed ice. Sprinkle a
little angostura on top of mixture after filling glasses.

PONCHE DE CRÈME (boiled) 242

6 eggs
1½-2 pt. cow's milk
½ lb. (1 cup) sugar
1½ pt. (3 nips) rum

2 oz. (6 tbsp.) cornstarch
vanilla essence to taste
wine, if liked
angostura bitters

Mix cornstarch with a little cold milk—boil the
remainder and add to cornstarch. Stir the two together
over the heat for 7 min. Cool and add beaten eggs.
Whisk and cook again until eggs thicken, but avoid

boiling, otherwise mixture will curdle. Add rum and essence. Keep in a cool place till required. Add crushed ice and angostura before serving.

243   GINGER BEER

2 oz. green ginger	juice and rind of 2 small
2 oz. cream of tartar	limes
1 gallon boiling water	1½ lb. sugar
¼ cake yeast	

Wash and pound ginger and add boiling water. Add juice and rind of limes, then cream of tartar. Cover but stir frequently. When lukewarm (tepid) add yeast dissolved in a little warm water. Mix well, cover, and leave to stand for 6 hours. Sweeten and bottle. Keep at least 3-4 days. Addition of a small quantity or rum makes it keep better.

244   MAWBY

1 heaped tbsp. mawby bark	3-4 cloves
	1 blade mace
small piece dried orange peel	6 pt. (12 glasses) cold water
½ in. piece of cinnamon	2 heaped cups sugar

Boil mawby, orange peel, cinnamon, clove, and mace in 1 cup water till strong—about 5 min. Cool, and add 6 pt. cold water and sugar. Add plenty of sugar, as the sweetness goes off during fermentation. Strain into bottles, filling to the shoulder only, so that entire neck of bottle is left for froth. Screw down and leave for about 3 days.

SORREL

There are two kinds—red and white. The drink prepared from the white sorrel is more acid, therefore more water should be allowed.

3 cups sorrel (heaped) without seeds	piece of ginger (½ inch square)
3 pt. (6 glasses) boiling water	piece of dried orange peel (1½ in. by ½ in.)
a few grains rice or barley	6 cloves
	1 lb. (2 cups) sugar

Wash sorrel, cut away seeds. Place in jar with ginger, orange peel, and cloves. Pour on boiling water, and allow to remain for 24 hr. Strain and sweeten. Pour into bottles, adding a few grains of barley or rice (this helps fermentation), and allow to remain for at least another day. Serve with ice.

17 Sauces

There are many different kinds of both sweet and savoury (salt) sauces—they are generally used for the following reasons:

1 To make food more nourishing—e.g. butter sauce may be served with white fish which contains little fat.
2 To moisten dry food—e.g. fried meat or steamed puddings are more tasty if served with sauce.
3 To improve flavour and so make food more appetising—e.g. a good tomato sauce can be served with reheated food.
4 To improve the appearance of food—e.g. steamed or boiled food which may be white and uninteresting looking is often coated with sauce.

Coating sauces must be made thicker than the flavouring sauces, which are poured from a sauce-boat.

246 CREOLE SAUCE OR GRAVY

1 tbsp. fat pork	½ tbsp. vinegar
1 tbsp. oil	1 teasp. salt (less if salt
1 tbsp. cooking butter	butter is used)
1 tomato	pepper to taste
1 small onion	½ tbsp. flour
2-3 blades chive	¼ pt. (½ glass) water
sprig of thyme	

Wash and slice seasonings. Wash and cut up fat pork, heat on a slow fire to melt out fat. Add oil and fry

seasonings lightly. Stir in flour, butter, and water. Boil
up and add vinegar and salt.

N.B. Flour and water are often omitted.

ORDINARY GRAVY
See recipe 97.

BREADNUT SAUCE 247

1 doz. breadnuts
1½ oz. (3 tbsp.) butter
½ oz. (2 tbsp.) flour

1 pt. (2 glasses) milk or
    white stock
pepper and salt to taste

Scald breadnuts, remove rind and skin, and pound them
till smooth. Melt butter, add nuts, and fry to a pale
brown. Stir in flour and stock and boil for 10 min., stirring
all the time.

GROUND-NUT OR CASHEW-NUT SAUCE 248

2 oz. (or about 1 cup)
    nuts
½ oz. (1 tbsp.) butter
½ oz. (2 tbsp.) flour

1 pt. (2 glasses) stock
pepper and salt to taste
pinch of sugar, if liked

Parch nuts, remove shell and brown skin, and pound or
mince finely. (Nuts may be fried instead of parched, if
preferred.) Melt butter, stir in flour, and fry to an even
brown. Add nuts, and gradually stir in stock. Boil 5 min.,
and skim, if necessary.

MOCK APPLE SAUCE 249
(To serve with pork, sucking pig, and duck)

about 3 green common
    mangoes
piece of lime peel

½ oz. (1 tbsp.) butter
½ oz. (1 tbsp.) sugar
¼ glass water

Wash, peel, and slice the mangoes. Cook them with the other ingredients till soft. Use a covered pan and stir occasionally. Take out the lime peel, and either sieve the mangoes or beat them with a wooden spoon. The sauce should be a thick purée. Serve hot.

250 WHITE SAUCE

FOR COATING

1 oz. (4 tbsp.) flour
1 oz. (2 tbsp.) butter $\Big\}$ to ½ pt. (1 glass) milk

FLOWING (TO POUR)

¾ oz. (3 tbsp.) flour
¾-1 oz. (1½-2 tbsp.) butter $\Big\}$ to ⅓ pt. (1 glass) milk

Melt butter in a small saucepan, add flour, and stir over the heat till butter is absorbed. (Don't let it turn brown.) Stir in milk, about one-third at a time. Boil up each time milk is added and stir all the time. Cook for not less than 5 min. Add pepper and salt to taste.

251 PARSLEY SAUCE

½ pt. white sauce   2 teasp. chopped parsley

Strip parsley from stalk and wash thoroughly. Dry it by squeezing tightly in a clean towel. Chop very finely. Make sauce and add parsley with salt, etc.

252 SHRIMP SAUCE

½ cup scalded shrimps
1½ oz. (3 tbsp.) butter
¾ oz. (3 tbsp.) flour
½ pt. (1 glass) milk

white pepper and salt to taste
squeeze of lime juice

Scald shrimps; remove skins and black cord down
centre of back; wash thoroughly; cut up if very large.
Heat butter, add shrimps, cover and cook until shrimps
are tender—about 7 min. Take out shrimps and add
flour. Continue as for white sauce. When sauce is ready
add shrimps and lime juice with salt, etc.

BREAD SAUCE 253

To serve with roast chicken or turkey, etc.

½ glass bread-crumbs	4 black peppers
½ pt. (1 glass) milk	(underground)
1 small onion	½ oz. (1 tbsp.) butter
2 cloves	½ teasp. salt

Peel onion but leave it whole. Put all ingredients except
bread-crumbs and butter into a saucepan. Heat to
boiling-point, keep covered and allow to stand 15 min.
to extract flavour of onion and clove. Strain. Add bread-
crumbs and butter. Re-heat and serve in a hot sauce-
boat.

MINT SAUCE 254

To serve with mutton

¼ pt. (½ glass) vinegar	½ tbsp. sugar
3 heaped tbsp. chopped	pinch salt
mint	2 tbsp. boiling water

Wash mint thoroughly. Dry well and remove stalks.
Chop finely. Mix sugar, salt, and mint in a sauce boat.
Add boiling water. When cold, add vinegar.

255   CREOLE PEPPER SAUCE—1

1 doz. red peppers	2 tbsp. salt
1 small green papaw	1½ pt. (3 glasses) vinegar
1 large onion	½ teasp. ground saffron
4 tbsp. mustard	1 teasp. curry powder
1-2 cloves garlic	

Boil papaw in skin, then cut into small squares or strips. Scald, stone, and mince or chop peppers. Mince onion and garlic. Mix all solid ingredients, add vinegar, and simmer mixture gently for 20 min. Cool, bottle, and label.

N.B. 1 cup boiled salad beans may be added if liked. (Remove hard edges and cut in half.)

256   CREOLE PEPPER SAUCE—2

8 strong peppers	1 onion (size of an egg)
¼ bottle vinegar	1 teasp. salt
Mustard	1 tbsp. olive oil

Wash and cut up peppers. Take out seeds. Cut onion into small pieces. Put everything into a saucepan and let it boil for 20 min.

257   PEPPERS IN SHERRY

about 6-10 bird peppers   about ¼ pt. (½ nip) sherry

Wash and dry peppers and add to sherry. Keep in a stoppered bottle. Use with soup, etc.

MANGO CHUTNEY—1   258

25 green mangoes	4 oz. salt
8 oz. currants	1 whole garlic or garlic to
4 oz. raisins	taste
8 oz. prunes or dates, if	2 red peppers
liked	2 pt. (4 glasses) vinegar
4 oz. green ginger	

Clean and stone raisins, dates, and currants. Mince or
chop them and mix with peppers and 1 pt. vinegar.
Leave to infuse for 24 hr. Peel and slice mangoes and
pound garlic. Mix all ingredients and boil to the desired
consistency. Stir frequently. Bottle and label.
N.B. Mangoes may be pounded with garlic if preferred.

MANGO CHUTNEY—2   259

1 doz. ripe mangoes	4 oz. (about 1½ cups)
8 oz. raisins	tamarind
4 oz. green ginger	8 oz. (1 cup) salt
1 whole garlic or garlic to	8 oz. (1 cup) sugar
taste	1 qt. (4 glasses) vinegar

Wash and peel mangoes and cut flesh into strips. Wash
and stone raisins. Peel and chop or pound garlic finely.
Peel and cut ginger into dice. Scrape tamarind and
discard seeds. Mix all solid ingredients. Boil vinegar,
pour over mixture, and stir well. Bottle and label.

Sweet sauces

260 COCONUT CREAM

about 1 cup grated   1 cup milk
  coconut

Heat the milk and pour it over the grated coconut. Let it
stand for about 5 min. then stir and squeeze it to extract
as much coconut fat and flavour as possible. Strain out
the coconut, pressing it well. Chill the cream before
serving.

261 BANANA SAUCE

2 medium-sized   ½ pt. (1 glass) water
  bananas
1 clove and a small bay ⎫
  leaf   ⎬ or other flavourings to
pinch cayenne pepper   taste
½ teasp. guava jelly   ⎭

Wash and peel bananas and put all ingredients in a
saucepan. Boil for 10 min., then sieve. Serve hot or cold.

262 CUSTARD SAUCE

1 egg yolk   ¼ pt. (½ glass) milk
1 teasp. sugar   flavouring to taste

Heat milk. Mix egg yolk and sugar and stir in the milk.
Strain into the saucepan and stir over a low heat until
custard thickens. Do not boil or custard will curdle. Add
flavouring. Serve hot or cold.
N.B. This sauce can only be made thicker by adding more
egg, longer cooking or boiling is useless.

JAM SAUCE

¼ pt. (½ glass) water
½ oz. (1 tbsp.) sugar
2 tbsp. jam or jelly
piece of lime peel

1 heaped teasp.
   arrowroot or
   cornstarch
squeeze of lime juice
colouring, if liked

Boil sugar, water, jam, and lime peel for 7 min. Strain or
simply remove peel. Mix arrowroot to a paste with a
little cold water, add to sauce and boil again for 3 min.,
stirring all the time. Add lime juice and colouring.

PEPPERMINT AND CHOCOLATE SAUCE
See ice-creams, chapter 14.

18 Using up scraps; re-heating food

Because heat destroys certain vitamins, raw food, or food only cooked for a short time, is more nourishing than food cooked twice, or for a long time. Heat also coagulates or hardens protein, and such things as meat may become dry with cooking because fat melts and water evaporates from it. Some vegetables are less nourishing after cooking, because boiling draws out the mineral salts. For these reasons the wise housewife tries to prepare just the right amount of food, so that no small pieces remain. Unfortunately this is not always possible, so we want to know the best way of using what is left over.

General rules

1 Make sure that the food is still fit to eat.
2 Add nourishment in the form of egg, milk, butter, gravy, etc., to make up for any loss in the first cooking.
3 Improve flavour with suitable seasonings or by adding some fresh food. Do not add any fresh food that requires long cooking.
4 Re-moisten the food.
5 Divide food into small pieces by mashing, mincing, or chopping, so that seasonings, moisture, etc, are well mixed up with the food, and so that it can be more easily made up into an attractive shape. While

doing this, remove all pieces of skin, gristle, bone, etc.

5 Never re-cook the food; quickly heat it for as short a time as possible.

Suggestions for using up scraps

Dry bread
Bake for rusks; use for stuffing; bread and butter pudding, cabinet pudding, queen of puddings; dry and crush for raspings, and use for coating fried foods, ham, etc.

Stale cake
Use for puddings.

Dry cheese
Toast or use for cheese pudding, macaroni cheese, cheese salad, etc.

Cooked potato
Mix with meat for beef balls, shepherd's pie. Use in a salad, for stuffing, potato bread, etc.

Cooked vegetables
Cooked vegetables, such as beans, peas, and carrots, can be used in a salad, or added to soup when it is cooked.

Boiled rice
Make into cakes and fry. Use for milk pudding, etc.

Cooked meat (beef, mutton, or fowl)
Use for pies, rissoles, eggs in ambush, mince, curry, pelau, fritters, savoury pancakes, jelly, stuffed vegetables (e.g. tomato, melongene).

Cooked fish
Use for fish balls, fritters, jelly (or cream), stuffed vegetables (e.g. christophine), Russian fish pie.

Bones
Use for stock, soup, or gravy.

264 MIXED RICE OR "COOK UP"

8 oz. cooked meat	½ teasp. salt—more if no
4 oz. salt meat, if liked	salt meat is used
1 lb. (2 cups) rice	½ teasp. pepper or piece
4½ cups water	green pepper
1 onion	2 tbsp. oil or dripping
1-2 tomatoes	1 heaped teasp.
2-3 blades chive	brown sugar
thyme and parsley	

Wash and soak salt meat and prepare seasonings. Heat the oil, add sugar, and fry till it bubbles. Add seasonings, fry till golden brown. Cut salt meat into neat pieces, and add to seasonings with water, rice, and salt; put to boil. Remove skin and bone from meat, cut into neat pieces, and add to rice when it is nearly cooked. If liked, add butter before dishing.

265 BEEF BALLS OR RISSOLES

8 oz. cooked meat	¼ teasp. black pepper
1-2 blades chive	8 oz. (2-3) cooked
small piece onion, if liked	potatoes, or ¼ pt. or
parsley and thyme	thick sauce or
1 small tomato	pananda
½ teasp. salt	

THICK SAUCE OR PANADA

1 teasp. Worcester
   sauce, if liked
2 tbsp. flour

1 tbsp. oil or butter
$\frac{1}{4}$ pt. ($\frac{1}{2}$ nip) water or stock

Prepare the seasonings and sauté (fry without browning) in a covered pot (this is because raw onion, etc., should not be mixed with cooked meat). If potatoes are used, mash and add salt if necessary. If a panada is used instead, melt the butter, add the flour, and gradually stir in the stock. Continue to stir and cook till smooth and very thick, so that it forms a ball in the pan. Cut away skin, gristle, and bone from the meat, and mince and chop it. Mix all ingredients, divide into required number of rissoles, and shape. Dip first in beaten egg or a thin batter, then coat with raspings or fresh bread-crumbs. Re-shape and press crumbs in place. Fry in smoking hot oil, following general rules for frying. Drain well. Serve on clean napkin.

DURHAM CUTLETS 266

Use the same mixture as for beef balls, but shape them like small cutlets or chops. When fried put a 1 in. piece of uncooked macaroni in the thin end of each to look like a cutlet bone.

EGGS IN AMBUSH 267

4-5 eggs
$\frac{1}{2}$ onion
small tomato
2-3 blades chive
parsley and thyme
1 teasp. salt
$\frac{1}{2}$ teasp. black pepper

4-5 sausages
or
1 lb. cooked meat and
   panada
or
8 oz. cooked meat and
8 oz. boiled potatoes

Hard boil and shell the eggs. Prepare seasonings, meat, and potatoes or panada (made as in recipe 265, but using 4 tbsp. flour, 2 tbsp. oil, $\frac{1}{3}$ pt. stock or water). If sausages are used, skin them. Divide mixture into 4-5 equal parts, and using a little flour, flatten out to a circle about $\frac{1}{2}$ in. thick. Use one part to enclose each egg, flatten slightly at each end. Coat and fry in the same way as beef balls. Cut in half and stand each piece with cut side upwards on a small circle of toast or fried bread. Serve hot or cold.

268 SHEPHERD'S PIE

8 oz. cooked meat	1 small tomato
about $\frac{1}{2}$ cup gravy or	parsley and thyme
stock	1 lb. (about 4-5) cooked
teasp. salt	Irish potatoes
$\frac{1}{4}$ teasp. black pepper or	1-2 tb p. oil or butter or
piece of green pepper	dripping
1 onion	1-2 tbsp. milk
1-2 blades chive	

Prepare seasonings and sauté (fry without browning) in a covered pan. Cut skin and bone from meat, and mice or chop it. Mix meat, seasonings, and gravy and place in a greased pie-dish. Mash potatoes, add milk, butter, and if necessary a little salt and pepper. Pile potato mixture over meat to form a crust. Smooth with a wet knife, then decorate. Brown quickly in a hot oven or under a grill—no real cooking is needed.

N.B. Some of the potato may be used to line the pie-dish, if liked.

269 FISH PIE

Make in the same way as Shepherd's Pie, using cooked fish instead of meat.

CURRY OF COLD MEAT OR FISH 270

pt. (1 nip) stock or
  coconut milk
onion
apple or mango or
  christophine
2 tbsp. flour
about 1 tbsp. curry or
  massala

1 tbsp. oil or dripping
$\frac{1}{2}$ teasp. salt
$\frac{1}{2}$ teasp. lime juice
1 teasp. chutney
1 lb. cooked meat or fish
rice
hot peppers to decorate

Prepare seasonings, fruit, and coconut milk. Heat oil,
lightly fry curry and then seasonings. Add flour,
christophine, chutney, lime juice, and coconut milk. Boil
up and skim well. Remove skin and bone from meat or
fish, and cut into neat pieces. Add it to the sauce and
heat it quickly without re-cooking. Serve on large dish
surrounded with a border of boiled rice and decorate
with pieces of red pepper.

STUFFED MELONGENE 271

about 1 cup cooked
  meat, minced or
  chopped
1 large melongene
1-2 tomatoes
3 tbsp. butter or dripping

$\frac{2}{3}$ cup bread-crumbs
1 teasp. salt
$\frac{1}{2}$ teasp. pepper
2-3 tbsp. raspings (dried
  crumbs)

Wash melongene and cut off a slice. Scoop out the
pulp, leaving a thin shell. Dice pulp and cook in butter or
dripping in a covered pan over low heat till soft. Chive
and onion may be cooked with the melongene, if liked.
Mix all ingredients except raspings and fill the shell.
Sprinkle top with raspings, add dabs of butter. Brown
quickly in a hot oven or under a grill—do not re-cook.

272   COOKED FISH OR SALMON CAKE

2 cups flaked cooked
   fish or dried salmon
1 cup bread-crumbs
1 cup milk
1 egg

2 tbsp. melted butter
1 teasp. lime juice
1 teasp. salt (less if
   salmon is used)
½ teasp. pepper

Remove skin and bone from fish, flake and measure it.
Beat egg lightly and add milk. Mix all ingredients. Turn
into a greased pie-dish. Bake in a quick oven till set.
Serve hot or cold.

273   RICE CAKES

2-3 cups boiled rice
1 egg

salt or sugar to taste

Lightly beat egg, and stir into the rice. Flavour to taste.
Form into neat cakes and fry till golden brown in
smoking hot oil. Drain well.

274   SALAD OF COOKED VEGETABLES

Use such things as cooked salad beans, carrot, Irish
potato, christophine, etc. These may be mixed with
lettuce and cress (after thorough washing), sliced
banana, chopped nuts, chopped raw onion.
Cut all ingredients into neat pieces and arrange in an
attractive way. Serve with Mayonnaise or French
Dressing, see Chapter 11, Green Vegetables.

See also the following recipes:
  85 Fish Fritters
139 Beef Pies
139 Stuffed Breadfruit

139 Fish Jelly
142 Russian Fish Pie
289 Savoury Custard

SALTED FISH (Tasa Sallé) 275

1 medium fish, e.g. king   about 10 tbsp. salt
   fish or mackerel

Remove head and bone the fish by cutting from the
back and separating flesh from the backbone. Do not
cut along the under-side (belly), as fish should remain in
one large piece. Remove bone and entrails. Wipe with a
wet cloth instead of washing. Using a sharp knife, make
slits lengthways on inner side of fish. Rub all over with
salt, working it well into the slits—use extra salt if
necessary. Place on a large dish and leave for one day.
Pour off brine solution which forms as fish stands. Wipe
with a clean cloth and dry in the sun—for several days if
necessary.
Keep in a clean dry place till required, and then scald
before using.

SOUSED MACKEREL OR RED FISH 276

1 large red fish   3 or 4 unground black
2-3 cloves   peppers or piece red
2 bay leaves   pepper
1 teasp. salt   about $\frac{1}{4}$ pt. ($\frac{1}{2}$ nip) vinegar
about $\frac{1}{4}$ pt. ($\frac{1}{2}$ nip) water

N.B. This will only keep 4 to 5 days.

Scale and bone the fish—cut into 2 or 4 fillets. Add salt

and roll fillets from head to tail. Place in a pie-dish, add all other ingredients, making certain that there is enough vinegar and water to cover the fish. Cover the dish and bake slowly for ¾ hr.

N.B. No onion, chive, or tomato should be used, otherwise the fish will not keep.

277 SMOKED MEAT

This method is best for fairly small pieces of meat. Unfortunately it makes it rather dry and tough. Clean meat and rub it well with plenty of salt. Hang it over a slow fire made from green wood; turn constantly until all sides are smoked. Leave it hanging over the place where a wood fire is used daily. When using part of the meat, cut from the lower end, so that the cut surface is quickly dried by the smoke.

TO PRESERVE MANGOES, PEPPERS, TOMATOES, ETC.
See recipes for Chutney, Hot Sauce, etc., in Chapter 17, Sauces.

278 CRYSTALLIZED SHADDOCK

Wash, dry, and grate off some of the green peel. Cut into strips about 1½ in. at the widest part. Soak in cold water for 12 hrs., changing the water several times, or better still leave under a slowly running tap—this removes bitter flavour. Put into fresh water and boil until soft. Colour during this stage if liked. Squeeze out all the water by twisting the strips.

Prepare a syrup by slowly dissolving 1½ lb. (3 cups) white sugar in ¾ pt. (1½ nips) water (do not stir). Simmer the peel in the syrup until it has all dried up (do not let it brown).

Prepare a second syrup using 1½ lb. (3 cups) sugar in ½ pt. (1 nip) water. Pour this hot over the peel, cover, and leave for a week or ten days. If syrup does not entirely cover peel, turn it daily, otherwise the exposed part will go mouldy. Drain and dry peel in the sun.

CANDIED PEEL   279

Neatly cut peel from about 6 oranges or lemons. Soak for 3-4 days in salt water made by dissolving ½ cup salt in 2 pt. (4 glasses) water. Drain well and boil until soft. Soak 12 hrs. in cold water to extract any salt that remains; change water two or three times.

Make a syrup by dissolving 3 lb. sugar in 1 pt. (2 glasses) water, then boil the peel in this until the syrup candies. Take out peel, sprinkle with fine sugar and dry before a fire, in a cool oven, or in the sun.

20 *Jams and jellies*

Everyone should know how to make jam and jelly, because quite often people have a large crop of fruit, such as guavas, plums, etc., which it is difficult to use up in any other way.

Choice of pan

1 Use a wide shallow pan. The jam will boil quickly and much steam will evaporate, so that the jam will jell (thicken) quickly without turning brown.
2 Use a thick pan: jam burns easily if the pan is thin.
3 Choose a suitable sized pan as jam boils over if the pan is too small.
4 Use a stainless steel pan if possible. Otherwise use enamelled iron (being certain that it is free from chips) or aluminium brightly polished before the fruit is put in.

Choice of sugar

Buy as good sugar as you can afford. Cheap sugar makes a lot of scum which has to be removed, and is therefore wasteful and non-labour-saving.

Choice of fruit

1 Use full but not ripe fruit. Slightly under-ripe fruit
   contains a gummy substance called pectin which
   helps the jam to jell. When ripe this pectin turns into
   a sugar called pectose.
2 Use sound, unbruised fruit.
3 Gather fruit on a dry day if possible: damp fruit may
   cause jam to go mouldy.

Preparation of fruit

1 Wash and drain, or wipe the fruit.
2 Discard any bruised or over-ripe fruit and remove
   stems, thick skins, etc.
3 Soak very acid fruit, e.g. tamarind, overnight. Next
   day cover with fresh cold water, heat to boiling-
   point, then throw away the water. Add a pinch
   bicarbonate (baking) soda, if liked.
4 Cut fruit into suitable sized pieces.

General rules for jam

1 Do not let jam boil until all sugar has dissolved.
2 Stir occasionally while boiling.
3 Skim when necessary.
4 Boil steadily: too fast boiling breaks the fruit, while
   too long boiling turns sugar brown.
5 When jam looks thick test it by putting a teaspoonful
   on a cold dry plate. Leave about 5 min. in a cool
   place, and if jam sets it is ready.
6 Bottle at once in clean dry warm jam jars (bottles). If

warm they are less likely to crack and more likely to
be dry. Stand them on something wooden while
filling.
7   Cover immediately with circles of clean waxed or
grease-proof paper. Cut a larger piece of paper or
cellophane to cover not only the top but the rim of
bottle. Damp one side of this and stretch over bottle
with damp side outwards. Tie down with fine twine.
As the paper dries it tightens. If liked, brush over
paper with white of egg or melted wax.
N.B. The old idea was to cool jam before covering.
This is bad as it allows germs, moulds, and dust to
enter. Cover jam while it is still steaming.
8   Label bottles stating kind of jam and date of making.
Store in a cool dry place.

Proportions and method for different fruits

Soft fruit (e.g. tomato)
Use no water. Allow 1 lb. sugar to every lb. fruit. Flavour
with spice. Place fruit in a wet pan and heat gently for
about 15 min. to extract a little juice. Add sugar and
follow general rules.

Firm fruit (papaw, pomme cythère, pmerac, plums,
mammy apple, etc.)
Flavour with ginger or spice. Break a few of the stones
and put back the kernel.
Allow half a pint of water to 6 lb. fruit, ¾ lb. sugar to every
lb. fruit. Dissolve sugar and water slowly. Add fruit and
follow general rules.

Hard fruit (pumpkin, googe, pineapple, etc.)
Flavour with the spice, ginger, or vanilla bean. Allow

about half as much water as fruit, ¾ lb. sugar to every lb. fruit. Boil fruit gently without sugar until nearly soft. Add sugar and follow general rules.

80 ORANGE MARMALADE

8 sour oranges	8 lb. sugar
juice of 2 limes	8 pt. water
juice of 2 sweet oranges	

Wash and peel oranges. Save peel and shred it finely. Slice fruit, remove seeds (pips), and soak them in half a pint of water. Soak fruit and peel overnight in remainder of the water. Strain water from seeds and add to fruit with lime and orange juice. Using the water in which fruit soaked, boil fruit and peel until the liquid has reduced to half. Add sugar and follow general rules for jam.

GRAPEFRUIT MARMALADE   281

1 large grapefruit	1 lemon
1 orange	5 lb. sugar

Wash fruit and slice thinly, discarding all seeds. Cover with 3 qt. of cold water and let stand until next day. Bring to boil slowly and boil 5 min. Remove from fire, add 5 lb. sugar, stirring until sugar is dissolved. Allow to stand in pan until next day. Boil slowly, and stir occasionally, until marmalade is thick and rich. This makes 7 lb. of marmalade.

General rules for jelly

1   Wash fruit and cut it up roughly—skins, seeds, etc.

should not be removed as these all make jelly, and will easily be removed while straining.

2   Cover fruit with water and boil till it has reduced to half.

3   Strain through a cloth. This should be tied to the legs of a chair or stool turned upside down on a table. If a really clear jelly is required let the juice drip, but if quantity rather than clearness is required squeeze the jelly cloth.

4   Allow 1 lb. sugar to every pint (2 glasses) strained juice.

5   Boil fast to preserve the colour.

6   Test and bottle in the same way as jam.

282   GUAVA JELLY

10 lb. guavas to make 4-5 pt. juice
4-5 lb. sugar
$\frac{1}{2}$ in. piece of alum to clear jelly and make it thicken quickly

283   TOMATO JELLY

use less water
add flavouring

284

APPLE JELLY

add grated rind of 1 lime

Meat and fish are relatively expensive, and for this reason some people become partial vegetarians. Other people are vegetarians because they dislike the idea of animals being killed for food, or because their religion does not allow them to eat any animal food.

The following foods are rich in protein and should be used plentifully:

Cheese	30-33 per cent. protein
Peanuts (ground-nuts)	25.8 per cent. protein
Dried beans	22.5 per cent. protein
Split peas	21.0 per cent. protein
Eggs	13.0 per cent. protein
Prunes and dates	4.3 per cent. protein
Milk	3.5 per cent. protein

GROUND-NUT CUTLETS 285

Sufficient to make 4 small cutlets

4 oz. nuts	¼ teasp. salt
4 tbsp. bread-crumbs	pepper to taste
small piece onion	¼ glass milk
1 small tomato	1 tbsp. butter } to bind
1 blade chive	2 tbsp. flour
½ teasp. chopped parsley	tomato or creole butter
few drops lime juice	sauce

Parch and shell nuts, then mince or pound them.
Prepare seasonings and lightly fry them in about 1 tbsp.

butter. Remove seasonings from butter and add flour. Stir in the milk, thus making a panada or very thick sauce for binding the ingredients together. Mix all ingredients, divide into four equal parts and shape as cutlets or rolls. Coat with egg and bread-crumbs or raspings. Fry in smoking hot oil till golden brown.

N.B. Cooked mashed potato may be used instead of the panada. The mixture may be made sweet instead of savoury.

286 LENTIL SOUFFLÉ

1 gill (½ glass) lentils or other legume (split peas, gubgub, etc.)	2 tbsp. butter seasonings to taste cream, if available
2 eggs	

Pick, wash, and soak lentils in about one and a half glasses water. Stew or steam them in the same water until soft, then sieve or beat them to a thick purée. Lightly fry any seasonings in a covered pot. Add butter, seasonings, cream, and egg yolks to lentils. Whisk egg whites very stiffly and fold them lightly into mixture. Pour into a greased pie-dish and bake in a moderate oven till set and well risen—about 20 min. Sprinkle with pepper. Serve at once before soufflé falls.

287 CURRIED EGGS

½ pt. (1 glass) coconut milk	2 tbsp. butter or oil
1 onion	½ teasp. salt
1-2 blades chive	½ teasp. lime juice
1 mango or piece of googe	1 teasp. chutney or hot sauce
	3-4 hard-boiled eggs

2 tbsp. flour
about 1 tbsp. curry or
    massala

rice
red peppers to decorate

Prepare seasonings, coconut milk, and eggs. Cut googe
or mango into neat pieces. Heat oil, lightly fry curry and
then seasonings. Add flour, googe, chutney, lime juice,
and coconut milk, boil up and skim well. Shell eggs and
re-heat in the sauce. (Eggs may be cut in half
lengthways if liked.) Place eggs on a hot dish. Coat with
sauce and arrange a border of rice.

N.B. Curried bananas may be prepared in the same way.

STUFFED EGGS   288

3 eggs
2 tbsp. butter
pepper and salt to taste
flavourings, e.g. one of the following:
    2-3 sardines or anchovies
    1 teasp. curry powder
    ½ teasp. marmite
    1 tbsp. finely grated cheese and ½ teasp. mustard,
        etc.
raspings
6 very small rounds bread and butter }
6 slices tomato   }   if liked

Boil eggs hard, turning them constantly at the start, so
that yolks do not set on one side. Shell eggs, cut in half,
and remove yolk. Wipe out these white cups of egg, cut
a small piece from the bottom so that they will stand
firmly, and decorate edge. Sieve or mash yolk, add
butter, pepper, salt, and prepared flavouring, and mix
thoroughly. Fill white cups using a fluting (icing) pipe or

teaspoon; pile mixture high. Add raspings if liked. Serve
on a bed of well washed salad, or decorate with parsley
or cress and stand on a slice of tomato on top of a small
round of bread and butter.

289   SAVOURY CUSTARD

2-3 eggs
1 pt. (2 glasses) milk
1 teasp. salt
pepper

1 teasp. chopped parsley
   or 2 tbsp. grated cheese
1 boiled onion

Prepare seasonings or cheese. Lightly beat eggs. Mix
all ingredients and pour into a greased pie-dish. Bake or
steam gently till set—about 45 min. Do not let custard
boil otherwise it will curdle (see Custard, recipe 66).
N.B. When not intended for a vegetarian, add about
half-cup flaked cooked or salted fish, or small pieces of
bacon or ham.

290   CHEESE PUDDING

½ glass fine bread-
   crumbs (with no
   crusts)
½ pt. (1 glass) milk
about 4 tbsp. grated
   cheese

2 tbsp. butter
1-2 eggs
salt and pepper to taste
½ teasp. dry mustard

Warm milk, add all ingredients except egg white. Whisk
egg white very stiffly, and fold lightly into mixture. Pour
into a greased pie-dish. Bake on the top shelf of a
moderate oven till set, well risen, and golden
brown—about 20-30 min. Serve at once before mixture
falls.

MACARONI CHEESE 291

3 oz. macaroni (or
  enough to cover the
  bottom of a 1 pt. pie-
  dish)
3 oz. (or about ½ cup)
  grated cheese
1 tbsp. butter
2 tbsp. flour

½ pt. (1 glass) milk, or ½
  glass milk and ½ glass
  macaroni water
½ teasp. mustard
½ teasp. salt
¼ teasp. pepper
slices of tomato or hard-
  boiled egg to decorate

Break macaroni into about 1½ in. pieces, wash and cook in boiling salted water till soft—about 20-30 min. Strain off water. Melt butter, add flour, and stir in milk, about one-third at a time. Boil up, stirring well. Add macaroni, salt, pepper, mustard, and about two-thirds of cheese. Pour into a greased pie-dish and sprinkle remainder of cheese on top. Brown in a hot oven as quickly as possible, decorate with tomato or hard-boiled egg.

CHEESE TARTLETS 292

2-3 oz. shortcrust pastry
¼ pt. (½ glass) milk
½ oz. (2 tbsp.) flour
½ oz. (1 tbsp.) shortening.

1-2 oz. (2-4 tbsp.) grated
  cheese
pepper and salt to taste
1 egg

Make pastry, roll out thinly, and line about 10-12 pie-pans. Prick bottom of each and set aside on ice. Grate cheese. Melt butter in a small saucepan and stir in flour without browning. Gradually beat in the milk and boil up, stirring all the time. Add cheese, pepper and salt, and egg yolk. Whisk egg white stiffly and fold lightly into cheese mixture. Half fill pastry cases and bake in a steady oven till well risen and golden brown—about 20 min. Serve at once before mixture falls.

22 *Some East Indian recipes*

The fats used in East Indian recipes are mostly in the form of ghee (butter) or coconut oil (see Chapter 6, Frying).

Indian foods are usually served rather dry and are very peppery, so it is necessary to know how to make good massala (curry paste).

293 MASSALA

6 tbsp. dhania
(coriander)
1 heaped teasp. souṅp
(anise seed)
1 heaped teasp. wuṅg
(cloves)
1 heaped teasp. hàrdi (or
colouring) saffron
1 heaped teasp. jira
1 heaped teasp. méthi

1 heaped teasp. gol
mirich (black pepper)
1 teasp. sarso (mustard
seed)—if to be used
for beef use double
quantity
3 cloves lesun (garlic)
1 large onion (piyaj)
lal mircha (red pepper) to
taste

Grind on a stone. Grind saffron first, adding enough water to make a stiff paste. Add all other ingredients by degrees, grinding very finely. Omit onion, garlic, and red pepper if it is to be kept overnight.

294 KALOUNJI

3 caraili (these are like
knobby cucumbers)

2 tbsp. massala
6 tbsp. oil

Wash caraili and cut along concave edge. Cut across if very large and remove seeds and tips. Heat oil in a deep pot till smoking and fry massala till brown. Use massala to stuff cavity in caraili. Fry caraili in a covered pot till soft and brown. Turn as required, being careful that stuffing does not fall out. Serve with rice, roti (bread), or bara (salt cake).

CARAILI CHOKA   295

Wash and slice caraili. Cover with salt for about half an hour. Squeeze well to extract salt and bitterness. Fry in smoking oil till soft and brown. Serve with roti, salt fish, etc.

BAIGAN (MELONGENE) CHOKA   296

Prepare as Caraili Choka (recipe 295).

ALU (POTATO) TALKARI   297

1 lb. (about 5 medium) potatoes	2 tbsp. coconut oil
1 teasp. salt	1 teasp. méthi
1 tbsp. massala	$\frac{1}{4}$ pt. ($\frac{1}{2}$ glass) water

Put oil to burn with méthi, strain and fry massala till light brown. Peel, wash, and slice potatoes, and add to massala with water and salt. Cover and simmer until potatoes are soft.

CHANA   (Chick peas or gram)   298

2 lb. (1 seer) chana peas	$\frac{1}{2}$ onion and a piece of red pepper
2 tbsp. massala	2 teasp. salt
4 tbsp. oil	

Soak peas overnight, then remove outer skin. Put in a

bowl and sprinkle with salt. Grind onion and pepper with massala and fry lightly in smoking hot oil. Add peas, cover, and fry till fairly soft, stirring constantly. Drain and serve with roti or rice.

299 BHAJI (Spinach)

2-3 bundles spinach	1 onion and a piece of
2 tbsp. coconut oil	red pepper
1 clove garlic	1 teasp. salt

Thoroughly wash and strip spinach. Pound or chop onion, garlic, and pepper. Burn oil, then brown onion, etc. Add spinach and salt—stir thoroughly. Cover and allow to steam in its own water. When nearly soft, open pot and allow water to dry off.

300 URDI OR WOOLLY PYROL WITH SAHINA
(Dasheen leaves)

2 bunches dasheen	1 tbsp. massala
leaves	2 tbsp. ghee
½ lb. (1 cup) urdi (small	
greenish black peas)	

Soak urdi overnight, then grind. Add massala. Wash and strip mid-ribs from leaves. Dry with a towel. Thinly spread back of leaf with urdi mixture, pack seven layers and roll. Slice into ¾ in. strips and fry. Drain and serve.
N.B. Use a special towel for wiping dasheen leaves as it will be sained.

DAL (OR DHOLL) 301

½ lb. (1 cup) split peas
   (matar ke dal)
small piece of saffron
   (about 1 in. long)
½ medium-sized onion

1 clove garlic or ½ teasp.
   jira
¾ pt. (1½ glasses) water
½ teasp. salt
1 tbsp. coconut oil

Pick, wash, and soak peas overnight. Next day boil with
saffron until soft. Add salt and chopped onion, then stir
with a fork and remove from heat. Burn the garlic or jira
in the coconut oil. Strain, add to peas, stir well, and
cover. After a few minutes when the flavour of the
burnt jira or garlic becomes pronounced, serve with
boiled rice. The dal should be of a medium consistency.

MURGI TALKARI (Curried chicken) 302

1 young chicken
1½ tbsp. massala
2 teasp. salt

2 tbsp. flour (or anta)
3½ tbsp. ghee or oil
¼ pt. (½ glass) water

Pluck, singe, clean, and joint chiden. Burn oil (if used)
with a clove of garlic and brown the massala. Coat joints
of chicken with flour and brown. Add rest of
ingredients, cover, and simmer until tender—about 45
min. Stir frequently. Enough water must be left to be
served as gravy.

MACHHALI KA TALKARI (Stewed fish) 303

1 lb. fish—or 1 medium-
   sized fish
1 tbsp. massala
½ onion
piece of red pepper
2 tbsp. flour

3-4 blades chive
1-2 tomatoes
1 teasp. salt
3 tbsp. oil
¼ pt. (½ glass) water

Grind massala, onion, and pepper. Wash and cut up chive and tomato. Trim, clean, and cut up fish. Sprinkle salt on fish and press on a mixture of flour and massala. Burn oil with a clove of garlic, remove the garlic and lightly fry seasonings, then the fish. Add water and simmer until soft—about 10-15 min.

304 GOS (Meat)

Cook in the same way as fish, adding 1 teasp. parched, ground jira seeds to gravy just before serving. Stew for an hour and a half.

305 PHULOURI

½ cup dal (or dholl) flour   2 teasp. salt
1 tbsp. massala   water to mix
    3 tbsp. oil

Prepare flour by washing and soaking split peas. Dry them and grind on a massala stone. Mix dal flour, salt, and massala with enough water to make a stiff dough. Knead lightly, shape into small balls, and fry in smoking hot oil. Drain well.

306 DAL PURI
Sufficient to make 6-7

½ lb. (1 cup) split peas   piece of red pepper
small piece saffron   1 lb. (4 cups) flour
1 teasp. jira   ½ teasp. bicarbonate
1 clove garlic   (baking) soda
½ onion   ½ teasp. salt

Pick and soak peas overnight. Next day boil with saffron till fairly soft. Parch and grind jira, add onion, garlic, pepper, and finally peas. Grind well. Sift flour, salt, and

soda. Add enough water to mix to a stiff dough. Form
into balls about the size of an orange, roll out to ½in.
thick, and put about 2-3 tbsp. dal mixture in the centre
of each circle. Fold over edges to cover dal and roll out
to ¼ in. again. Place on hot greased baking-stone, daub
with ghee or paper saturated with oil. Turn constantly.
Cook till brown and puffy—about 10 min.

PARATHA   (Roti with ghee)   307

½ lb. (2 cups) flour   ¼ teasp. salt
¼ teasp. bicarbonate   milk to mix
  (baking) soda

Sift flour, soda, and salt together. Add enough milk to
mix to a stiff dough. Form into balls about the size of a
small egg—flatten each with a rolling-pin or bottle.
Daub with ghee, then fold into a ball again. Roll out,
cook on a hot baking-stone. (Baking-stone should be
previously heated and tested by sprinkling with flour
which should brown within a few seconds.) Turn
constantly while cooking and spread plentifully with
butter.

BARA   (Indian salt cake)   308

4 tbsp. dal flour   pinch bicarbonate
2 tbsp. white flour   (baking) soda
1 tbsp. massala   ½ teasp. salt
                                 water to mix

Prepare dal flour as for Phulouri. Sift all dry ingredients
together, add massala and mix to a stiff dough with
water. Shape into a ball and roll out to a circle about 5 in.
across and ¼ in. thick. Fry in smoking hot oil till golden
brown. Drain well.

309   **MOHAN BHOG**   (Sweet cake)

½ lb. (2 cups) flour
¼ teasp. bicarbonate
(baking) soda, or 2
teasp. baking powder
1 teasp. ground spice
and clove mixed

4 tbsp. munaka (raisins)
¼ lb. (½ cup) sugar
goat's milk or water to
mix
3-4 tbsp. ghee

Parch flour in a dry iron pot till pale gold colour, turning
constantly. Pick and wash raisins. Sift flour, soda, and
spice; add sugar and raisins. Using a wooden spoon,
mix to a dropping consistency with goat's milk. Heat
ghee till smoking, stir in mixture, and cook until ghee is
absorbed—about 5 min. Cool slightly, mould, and when
cold, cut in slices.

N.B. For special cakes use equal parts rice flour and
white flour. To make rice flour, steam white rice, dry
thoroughly and grind finely.

310   **GULGULA**

1 lb. (4 cups) flour
1 teasp. dal chini (ground
spice)
2-3 eggs (anda)

about ½ cup milk
4 teasp. baking powder
about 6 oz. (1 cup) raisins
1 lb. (2 cups) sugar

Sift flour and spice into a bowl, add eggs and enough
milk to mix to a stiff paste. Beat thoroughly. Add raisins,
baking powder, and half sugar, and mix well. Form into
a roll on a flour board, cut off 1 in slices and dip each in
remaining sugar. Fry in smoking hot oil till golden brown
and cooked through. Sugar again or soak for a short
time in thick syrup.

JILEBI (Fried yeast mixture)   **311**

1 lb. (4 cups) flour	about $\frac{1}{2}$ pt. (1 glass)
$\frac{1}{4}$ oz. yeast or piece of	warm water
baker's dough (leaven)	thick sugar syrup made
2 teasp. sugar for yeast	by boiling 1 lb. (2 cups)
spice, if liked	sugar, $\frac{1}{2}$ pt. (1 glass)
	water and spice

Mix yeast and sugar. Sift flour and add to yeast with
enough warm water to make a thick batter. Leave to
rise overnight. Next day beat lightly and add enough
water to make it of a pouring consistency. Prepare a pot
of smoking hot ghee or oil. Pour mixture into ghee
through a funnel or tin cup with a small hole in the
bottom. Form rings by circling pan 3 or 4 times. Fry till
golden brown. Drain and soak in hot syrup for 5-7 min.
When cool the syrup must not remain sticky, but dry
with a sugary coating.

THE IDEAL CHAPATTI (Diet)   **312**
Taken from an Indian paper

Nutrition Research: One Anna Recipe
A recipe for a nutritious chapatti suitable for outdoor
workers in India has been evolved by the Nutrition
Research Laboratories at Coonoor. A manual labourer
needs at least two good meals a day. It is often
impossible for him to return home to consume his
midday meal, and he cannot afford to eat it in a hotel
even if one were available. The meal, therefore, which
he takes with him, should be sufficient in quantity and
well balanced—that is, it should contain the essential
nutritive elements in correct proportions. It should be
cheap, made of easily obtainable foods and be simple to
prepare. It should be easy to carry, that is, it should be

solid to avoid the possibility of spilling, small in bulk, and
not require a special utensil to contain it, and should also
remain fresh and palatable for a number of hours.

THE INGREDIENTS

Such a missi chapatti fulfilling all these conditions may
be made from the following ingredients: Wholewheat,
10 oz. or 5 chataks, Bengal gram flour (chana pea flour),
$2\frac{1}{2}$ oz. or $1\frac{1}{4}$ chataks, onions, $\frac{3}{4}$ oz. or $\frac{3}{8}$ chatak; fenugreek
leaves (or any other green edible leaves), $\frac{1}{2}$ oz. or $\frac{1}{4}$
chatak, milk, 1 oz. or $\frac{1}{2}$ chatak; salt, $\frac{1}{2}$ oz. or $\frac{1}{4}$ chatak, and
ghee or butter, $\frac{1}{4}$ oz. or $\frac{1}{8}$ chatak.

These consituents, except ghee, are mixed, water
being added and the whole kneaded into a dough.
Chapattis are made from the dough in the ordinary way
good thick chapattis being recommended, since these
remain fresh longer than the thin ones. Subsequently
ghee is smeared on the chapattis. The weight of this
meal is about 1 lb. or half a seer; it will supply about
1,300 to 1,400 calories, which is approximately half the
daily requirement of a labourer, and about 50 grammes
of protein.

The mixture contained in the chapattis is rich in
vitamin and mineral salts. If fresh milk cannot be
obtained, khoa or skimmed milk powder can be used.
For those who can afford it, the addition of a greater
quantity of milk or an egg to the dough is
recommended.

Chinese dishes

Some general hints

1 Use soya bean oil except for noodles, which require lard. Soya bean oil is a good source of vitamin.
2 Use cornflour (cornstarch) for thickening in the proportion of $\frac{1}{2}$ oz. ($1\frac{1}{2}$ tbsp.) to $\frac{1}{2}$ pt. (1 large cup) water.
3 Season with Shee Yow instead of salt—a special quality may be bought for table use.
4 Soak all dried vegetables:
   Mushrooms—cold water 1 hour, then remove stems
   Gum choy (lily petals)—hot water 15 min.
   Wun Yee (cuplike fungus)—hot water 15 min.
   Chungchow (parsnip)—hot water 10 min.
   Lin ny yow koy (lotus roots)—hot water 20 min.
5 Serve food straight from the heat—people often wait while it is being cooked.

N.B. A particular point about Chinese food is its long preparation and very short cooking; this should make it nourishing as there is little loss of vitamin.

313   PORK SOUP WITH CHINESE VEGETABLES

1 lb. lean pork
2 oz. foo chook (dried
   bean curd)
2 oz. dried mushrooms
1 onion
2-3 blades chive
1 teasp. pepper

1 tbsp. shee yow
1 teasp. ve tsin (gourmet
   powder)
3½ pt. (7 glasses) cold
   water
2 young see quar
   (quiquee)

Soak bean curd 30 min. if fresh, overnight if dark and old. Soak mushrooms 1 hr. Clean, cut up (1 in. long, ¼ in. thick), and season pork, using shee yow instead of salt. Simmer pork, bean curd, and mushrooms 1½hrs. Wash and peel see quar (it should not strip along the edges for this shows that it is old). Cut in half lengthways, then across diagonally in 1 in. blocks. Add it to soup 5 min. before removing from heat.

314   JAN SIN YU
(Steamed fish with mixed vegetable dressing)

1 lb. fish (grouper is best)
½ oz. gum choy (lily petals)
½ large onion or ½ oz. spring onions
½ oz. fresh ginger   } cut into fine
¼ oz. chung choy (dried parsnip   } pieces
leaves)
2 large mushrooms (dried)
1 tbsp. shee yow
1 teasp. salt
1 tbsp. cornflour water

Soak lily petals, mushrooms, and parsnip in the usual way. Remove hard ends from lily petals and chop

vegetables finely. Clean fish, wash with lime juice, and place in a steamer with a piece of greaseproof paper or a dish at the bottom. Mix vegetables with remaining ingredients except ginger and put over fish. Steam until firm—about 20-30 min. Add peeled and sliced ginger half way through the steaming. Serve at once.
N.B. 1½ oz. pork cut into fine slices can also be added.

STEAMED CHICKEN   315

1 fat chicken, about 3 lb.	2 tbsp. shee yow
6 cloves garlic	1 teasp. ng heung foon
3 teasp. salt	(spice powder)

Pluck, singe, and clean chicken in the usual way, but do not cut it up. Pound garlic and salt to paste, add shee yow and spice powder. Rub chicken well with this mixture both inside and out. Turn wings underneath, and place chicken breast upwards in a steamer or in a tightly covered pan containing very little water. Steam till tender—about 1½-2 hrs. Serve with mixed vegetables, which may be cooked at the same time:

1½ bamboo shoots (could be obtained canned)	½ oz. chung choy (preserved parsnips in bundles)
2 oz. water chestnuts	
1 oz. mushrooms	¼ oz. ginger (fresh)
¼ oz. wun yee (lichen)	½ oz. gum choy (lily petals)
	4 hung jo (jujube fruits)

Cut all ingredients into very fine pieces. Mix together with a little salt, pepper, sugar, sesame oil, cooking sherry, soya sauce, and cornflour water. Place on top of the chicken (20 min. before serving).

316   NG HEUNG JA GAI   (Fried spiced chicken)

1 young chicken, about 4 lb.	½ teasp. ng heung foon (Chinese spice)
½ teasp. salt	¼ teasp. pepper
	4 tbsp. gin

Pluck, singe, and clean chicken in usual way. Remove head and lower leg and wing joints. Cut into four pieces, *i.e.* cut in half each way. Mix all ingredients and leave to soak with chicken for 12 hrs. Half-fill a deep pot with oil. Fry chicken in smoking hot oil till golden brown and tender—about 30 min. (allow 1 hr. if chicken is whole). Use a slow heat and avoid over-heating oil. Baste chicken if not covered with oil. When cooked cut chicken into pieces about 1 in. long and ½ in. wide. Place in a dish and sprinkle spicery salt on the top.

317   PORK WITH FOO CHOOK AND KIM CHIM

2 oz. foo chook (dried bean curd)	1 lb pork or chicken
2 oz. kim chim (dried lily)	1 tbsp. shee yow (salt sauce)
2 tbsp. soya bean oil	½ teasp. salt
	½ teasp. pepper

Soak bean curd overnight in cold water or for 20 min. in boiling water. Soak dried lily ½ hr. in boiling water. Clean and cut pork into neat pieces—about 1 in. cubes. Season with salt, pepper, and shee yow. Brown pork in hot oil and add about ½ pt. (1 glass) water. Add bean curd, cover, and simmer 1 hr. Add dried lily, cook for another ½ hr., when all ingredients should be tender.

CHOP SUEY

6 oz. chicken meat ⎫
3 oz. onions ⎪
½ oz. mushrooms ⎪
½ oz. bamboo shoots ⎬ cut into fine slices
½ oz. celery ⎪
4 oz. bean sprouts ⎪
3 oz. tomatoes ⎭
1 egg well beaten

Scald tomatoes and remove skins. Soak mushrooms, remove stalks, and slice finely. Wash and pick bean sprouts. Place chicken in a hot oiled pan and cook for 1 min. Add bamboo shoots, bean sprouts, onions, celery, mushrooms, and salt to taste. Cook for 1 min. Add tomatoes and cook for 2 min. Add a little cornflour water, a few drops of sesame oil and soya sauce (shee yow) and a ¼ teasp. sugar (add noodles if desired), and cook all together for 1 min. Add a dash of rum or Worcester Sauce, if liked. Place in dish and keep hot. Put beaten egg in a hot oiled pan and cook for 2 min. Place omelette over the Chop Suey and serve.

N.B. Lobster meat or pork may be substituted for chicken, and ½ oz. fun si (corn noodles) may be added to recipe. To prepare the latter, place corn noodles in a saucepan of boiling oil and cook for 3 min., then take out and add to chop suey with the cornflour water. 1 or 2 carrots, cristophines, or cabbage leaves may also be added, if liked.

319   **SEY FOO GNAR CHOY**   (Bean sprouts with tomatoes)

2 portions gnar choy
(bean sprouts)
¾ lb. (about 4 good sized
tomatoes
½ onion (or ½ oz. spring
onions) cut into 1½ in.
slices)

1 teasp. salt
3 tbsp. stock or water
2 tbsp. cornflour
(cornstarch) water
¼ lb. pork if liked (cut in
very thin slices)
about 4 tbsp. oil

Scald and skin tomatoes, and cut in half. Remove roots
from bean sprouts, and wash thoroughly. Slice onion.
Clean and chop pork. Heat oil in a deep pot; when
smoking pour off all except for about ½ tbsp. Brown
pork. Add bean sprouts and toss for 1 min. Add stock or
water, cover, and steam 2 min. Add salt, onion, and
tomatoes, and toss again for 1 min. Add cornflour water
and cook 3 min. Serve at once.

N.B. Good bean sprouts are pale and short. Sprouted
peas may be used instead. Celery may be added, if
liked.

320   **STEAMED EGGS WITH HAMMI**

4 eggs
3 oz. hammi (dried
shrimps)
1 cup water

½ teasp. pepper
½ tbsp. shee yow
½ oz. spring onions.

Wash dried shrimps and soak for ½ hr.; chop finely. Beat
eggs and add all other ingredients. Pour into a greased
bowl and steam till set—about ½ hr.

POW CHOY AND WUN YEE (Cabbage and wun yee) 321

5 tbsp. oil	1 oz. pork
1 lb. cabbage	$\frac{1}{4}$ cup cornstarch water
2 oz. wun yee	1 tbsp. shee yow

Soak cabbage 15 min. in salted water. Throw away discoloured parts and stalk. Cut into $\frac{1}{2}$ in. slices, then across so that it is more or less in squares. Soak wun yee in hot water for 15 min., then pick off woody pieces. Chop the pork in very thin slices. Heat oil in deep pot. Pour off all except for $\frac{1}{2}$ tbsp. Toss cabbage and wun yee in pot for about 2 min. Add all other ingredients, cover, and steam in its own water for 5 min.

N.B. More pork can be added as in previous recipe, if liked.

CRISTOPHINE AND WUN YEE 322

2 cristophines	$\frac{1}{4}$ teasp. pepper
1 lb. pork	2 tbsp. soya bean oil
$1\frac{1}{2}$ tbsp. shee yow	$\frac{1}{2}$ cup cornflour water
1 oz. wun yee	

Soak and thoroughly pick wun yee. Peel and cut christophine into straws. Clean, chop,. and season pork with 1 tbsp. shee yow and pepper. Heat oil and brown pork quickly. Add cornflour water, remaining $\frac{1}{2}$ tbsp. shee yow and wun yee. Simmer 10 min., stirring often. Add cristophine and cook again for 15 min.

24 *Miscellaneous recipes*

323 CONQUINTAY FLOUR

Take full green plantains, peel and slice thinly lengthways. Lay slices on a board and dry in the sun, turning occasionally. When quite dry and crisp—about 4-5 days—pound while warm from the sun and sift through muslin. Use for bakes, coo-coo, etc.

324 FOO FOO OR POUND PLANTAIN

Boil 4-5 green plantains without salt. When soft, cool, peel, and pound them in a wooden mortar. Dip pestle in cold water frequently, otherwise plantain will stick. When plantain forms a smooth ball, re-heat, season, and serve it with Creole soups.

325 STUFFING OR FORCEMEAT

½ cup fresh bread-
    crumbs
    cracker crumbs
    cooked mashed
    potato   use one of these or a
    cooked mashed   mixture of two of
    chatigne   them
    farine

2 tbsp. butter or chopped suet or fat pork
2 teasp. chopped parsley
2-3 sprigs of thyme

tbsp. chopped onion or chive   if liked
chopped tomato
teasp. pepper or piece of red pepper
teasp. salt
beaten egg or milk to bind

This can be used for chicken, turkey, fish, etc.
Prepare all ingredients, removing stalks from parsley
and thyme. Mix all dry ingredients. Add enough egg,
milk, or water to bind them firmly together—use as
required.

CHOW CHOW   326

Wash, peel, and slice full but unripe mangoes. Sprinkle
with pepper and salt and add about 1 tbsp. vinegar to
every 2-3 mangoes. Serve with meat or fish.

VANILLA ESSENCE   327

Soak 2-3 vanilla pods in $\frac{1}{2}$ pt. (1 nip) rum.
A strong essence is more economical as less will be
required for flavouring.

HOME-MADE VINEGAR   328

Plain 'acid water' made from acetic acid and water is not
a good substitute for vinegar. Used regularly it is
definitely harmful.

Cane juice vinegar
Allow juice to ferment for 4-5 weeks. Strain and colour
with a little burnt sugar.

2 *Gingerbeer and Mawby vinegar*
Ferment liquid for 1-2 weeks.

3 *Molasses vinegar*
4 pt. (8 glasses) molasses
6 gallons soft water
½ oz. yeast

Stand mixture in a warm place for 3 weeks. Strain and bottle.

Index of recipes

Numbers refer to pages